Perfect PASTA

Pasta is versatile, economical and best of all good for you. The ways it can be served and the forms it comes are almost limitless as the recipes in this book show you. Most of the recipes are quick and easy to prepare making them ideal for weekday meals. Whether it's a substantial main meal, a quick lunch or a hearty winter soup that you are looking for you are sure to find a recipe to suit the occasion.

CONTENTS

THE PANTRY SHELF

Unless otherwise stated the following ingredients used in this book are:

Cream — Double, suitable for whipping

Flour — White flour, plain or standard

Sugar — White sugar

WHAT'S IN A TABLESPOON?

NEW ZEALAND
1 tablespoon =
15 mL OR 3 teaspoons

UNITED KINGDOM
1 tablespoon =
15 mL OR 3 teaspoons

AUSTRALIA
1 tablespoon =
20 mL OR 4 teaspoons

The recipes in this book were tested in Australia where a 20 mL tablespoon is standard. All measures are level.

The tablespoon in the New Zealand and United Kingdom sets of measuring spoons is 15 mL. In many recipes this difference will not matter. For recipes using baking powder, gelatine, bicarbonate of soda, small quantities of flour and cornflour, simply add another teaspoon for each tablespoon specified.

SOUPS

Soups made with pasta are hearty, healthy and satisfying. While any type of pasta can be used in soup, the smaller shapes are the most popular. A good way to use odds and ends of pasta you may have in the cupboard is to add them to soup.

Spaghetti Basil Soup

SPAGHETTI BASIL SOUP

155 g/5 oz spaghetti, broken into pieces
2 tablespoons vegetable oil
1 onion, chopped
2 cloves garlic, crushed
60 g/2 oz slivered almonds
4 cups/1 litre/1³/₄ pt chicken stock
30 g/1 oz fresh basil leaves, shredded
freshly ground black pepper

1 Cook spaghetti in boiling water in a large saucepan following packet directions. Drain and set aside.

2 Heat oil in a large saucepan and cook onion, garlic and almonds, stirring over a medium heat for 6-7 minutes or until onions are transparent.

3 Add stock and basil to pan and bring to the boil, reduce heat, cover and simmer for 10 minutes. Stir in spaghetti and season to taste with black pepper. Spoon soup into bowls and serve immediately.

Serves 4

Sprinkled with Parmesan cheese and served with bread rolls this soup makes a wonderful summer lunch dish. Basil gives it its distinctive flavour.

MINESTRONE

315 g/10 oz dried white beans
6 cups/1.5 litres/2¹/₂ pt water
6 cups/1.5 litres/2¹/₂ pt chicken stock
125 g/4 oz mushrooms, sliced
155 g/5 oz green beans, chopped
2 carrots, chopped
2 zucchini (courgettes) sliced
1 leek, sliced
155 g/5 oz small shell pasta
440 g/14 oz canned tomatoes, undrained and mashed
freshly ground black pepper
grated Parmesan cheese

1 Place dried beans and 4 cups/1 litre/1³/₄ pt water in a large bowl, cover and set aside to soak for 8 hours or overnight.

2 Drain beans and rinse in cold water. Place beans and stock in a large saucepan, bring to the boil and boil for 10 minutes, then reduce heat, cover and simmer for 1 hour or until beans are tender.

3 Add mushrooms, green beans, carrots, zucchini (courgettes), leek and remaining 2 cups/500 mL/16 fl oz water to pan. Bring to the boil, then reduce heat, cover and simmer for 30 minutes. Stir pasta and tomatoes into soup and cook for 10 minutes longer or until pasta is tender. Season to taste with black pepper. Sprinkle with Parmesan cheese and serve immediately.

Serves 6 as a main meal

Served with crusty bread and a glass of wine, Minestrone is a meal in itself.

Italian Chicken Soup

ITALIAN CHICKEN SOUP

12 cups/3 litres/5 pt chicken stock
4 chicken breast fillets, skinned
1 teaspoon whole black peppercorns
4 bay leaves
1 sprig fresh rosemary
1 onion, chopped
1 red pepper, chopped
2 carrots, chopped
185 g/6 oz short pasta shapes,
such as macaroni
250 g/8 oz cabbage, shredded
2 tablespoons grated Parmesan cheese

1   Place stock in a large saucepan and bring to the boil. Add chicken breasts, peppercorns, bay leaves and rosemary. Reduce heat, cover and simmer for 20 minutes or until chicken is just cooked.

2   Using a slotted spoon, remove chicken from pan and set aside to drain. Strain stock and return liquid to a clean saucepan. Add onion, red pepper, carrots and pasta to stock, cover, then bring to simmering and simmer for 20 minutes or until pasta is cooked and vegetables are tender.

3   Slice chicken. Stir chicken and cabbage into soup and cook for 5 minutes longer. Just prior to serving, stir in Parmesan cheese.

Serves 6

This clear chicken broth made with fresh chicken and vegetables makes a nutritious and delicious light meal that any weight watcher will love.

SPINACH SOUP

4 cups/1 litre/1^3/4 pt chicken stock
60 g/2 oz small pasta shapes
250 g/8 oz frozen chopped spinach, thawed
freshly ground black pepper
2 egg yolks

1   Place stock in a large saucepan and bring to the boil. Add pasta and spinach and cook, stirring occasionally, for 10 minutes or until pasta is tender. Season to taste with black pepper.

2   Place egg yolks in a small bowl and whisk to combine. Whisk a little hot soup into egg yolks, then stir egg yolk mixture into soup. Serve immediately.

Serves 6

VERMICELLI ONION SOUP

60 g/2 oz butter
3 onions, thinly sliced
1 tablespoon flour
1^1/4 cups/315 mL/10 fl oz hot chicken stock
4 cups/1 litre/1^3/4 pt milk
60 g/2 oz vermicelli, broken into pieces
freshly ground black pepper

1   Melt butter in a large saucepan and cook onions, stirring, over a medium heat for 6-7 minutes or until soft. Stir in flour, then gradually stir in hot stock. Cook, stirring constantly, for 4-5 minutes or until soup is smooth and thickened.

2   Stir in milk and bring to the boil. Add vermicelli and season to taste with black pepper. Cook, stirring frequently, for 8-10 minutes or until vermicelli is tender.

Serves 6

Vermicelli Onion Soup

CHILLI CHICKEN SOUP

100 g/3¹/₂ oz fresh egg noodles
2 tablespoons peanut oil
2 onions, chopped
2 cloves garlic, crushed
1 red chilli, finely sliced
1 teaspoon curry paste (vindaloo)
¹/₄ teaspoon ground turmeric
1 tablespoon finely chopped
fresh lemon grass or 1 tablespoon
finely grated lemon rind
4 cups/1 litre/1³/₄ pt coconut milk
1¹/₂ cups/375 mL/12 fl oz chicken stock
375 g/12 oz cooked chicken, chopped
3 spinach leaves, finely shredded

1 Cook noodles in a large saucepan of boiling water for 3-4 minutes or until tender. Drain, then rinse noodles under cold running water. Drain again and place in individual bowls.

2 Heat oil in a large saucepan and cook onions for 2-3 minutes or until golden. Stir in garlic, chilli, curry paste, turmeric and lemon grass, and cook for 1 minute.

3 Combine coconut milk and chicken stock. Add coconut milk mixture, chicken and spinach to pan. Bring to simmering and simmer for 3-4 minutes. Spoon soup over noodles in bowls and serve immediately.

Serves 6

Coconut milk can be purchased canned, or as a long-life product in cartons, or as a powder to which you add water. These products have a short life once opened and should be used within a day or so.

Chilli Chicken Soup

You can make coconut milk using desiccated coconut and water. To make, place 500 g/1 lb desiccated coconut in a bowl and pour over 3 cups/750 mL/1¹/₂ pt of boiling water. Leave to stand for 30 minutes, then strain, squeezing the coconut to extract as much liquid as possible. This will make a thick coconut milk. The coconut can be used again to make a weaker coconut milk.

Italian Bean Soup

ITALIAN BEAN SOUP

1 tablespoon olive oil
2 onions, chopped
2 cloves garlic, crushed
1 red pepper, chopped
6 cups/1.5 litres/2^1/$_2$ pt chicken or
vegetable stock
125 g/4 oz small pasta shapes
^{1}/$_2$ cup/125 mL/4 fl oz red wine
440 g/14 oz canned tomatoes, undrained
and mashed
2 tablespoons tomato paste (purée)
315 g/10 oz canned red kidney beans,
drained
freshly ground black pepper

1   Heat oil in a large saucepan and cook onions, garlic and red pepper for 4-5 minutes or until onion softens.

2   Stir in stock, pasta, wine, tomatoes, tomato paste (purée) and beans. Bring to the boil, then reduce heat and simmer for 15 minutes. Season to taste with black pepper.

Serves 6

Thick soups made with pulses and pasta are true peasant food. But they are just as good for filling hungry teenagers.

STARTERS

Pasta makes a light and appetising first course, but remember not to serve too much or you will not be able to eat the rest of your meal. For a starter, allow about 75 g/2^1/2 oz per serve. These recipes also make great light meals, just increase the serving size and add a salad.

Caviar Fettuccine

CAVIAR FETTUCCINE

300 g/9$^1/_2$ oz fettuccine
2 tablespoons olive oil
2 cloves garlic, crushed
2 tablespoons finely snipped fresh chives
3 tablespoons red caviar
3 tablespoons black caviar
2 hard-boiled eggs, chopped
4 tablespoons sour cream

Serves 4

1   Cook fettuccine in boiling water in a large saucepan following packet directions. Drain, set aside and keep warm.

2   Heat oil in a large frying pan and cook garlic over a low heat for 3-4 minutes. Add fettuccine, chives, red and black caviar, and eggs to pan. Toss to combine. Serve immediately, topped with sour cream.

A truly elegant starter. This colourful dish only takes minutes to prepare and is sure to be a hit at any dinner party.
If your budget does not run to caviar, this recipe is also delicious made with red and black lumpfish roe.

BLUE CHEESE PENNE

500 g/1 lb penne

BLUE CHEESE SAUCE
1 cup/250 mL/8 fl oz cream (double)
185 g/6 oz blue cheese, crumbled
3 tablespoons grated fresh
Parmesan cheese
freshly ground black pepper

Serves 6

1   Cook penne in boiling water in a large saucepan following packet directions. Drain, set aside and keep warm.

2   To make sauce, place cream and blue cheese in a saucepan, bring to the boil, stirring constantly, over a medium heat. As soon as the mixture reaches the boil, remove from heat and pour over pasta. Sprinkle with Parmesan cheese, season to taste with black pepper and toss to combine. Serve immediately.

This recipe is also wonderful using macaroni or bow pasta in place of the penne.

FUSILLI WITH ROSEMARY SAUCE

500 g fusilli or spiral pasta
1 tablespoon olive oil
2 cloves garlic, crushed
2 teaspoons finely chopped fresh
rosemary or 1 teaspoon dried rosemary
440 g/14 oz canned tomatoes, drained
and mashed
freshly ground black pepper
60 g/2 oz grated mozzarella cheese

Serves 6

1   Cook pasta in boiling water in a large saucepan following packet directions. Drain, set aside and keep warm.

2   Heat oil in a frying pan and cook garlic and rosemary, over a low heat, for 2-3 minutes. Add tomatoes, bring to simmering and simmer for 3-4 minutes. Season to taste with black pepper. Add pasta to tomato sauce and toss to combine. Serve immediately, topped with mozzarella cheese.

A native of the Mediterranean shores, rosemary is an extremely aromatic herb, much used by Italian cooks. It is easy to grow, but requires a sunny protected position with good drainage. In cold climates rosemary is best cultivated in a container so that it can be moved to the protection of a glasshouse in winter.

Fettuccine with Coriander Sauce

500 g/1 lb fettuccine

CORIANDER SAUCE
2 cloves garlic, chopped
60 g/2 oz walnut pieces
60 g/2 oz fresh coriander leaves
15 g/^{1}/$_{2}$ oz fresh parsley leaves
4 tablespoons vegetable oil
60 g/2 oz grated Parmesan cheese
freshly ground black pepper

1   Cook fettuccine in boiling water in a large saucepan following packet directions. Drain, set aside and keep warm.

2   To make sauce, place garlic, walnuts, coriander and parsley in a food processor or blender and process to finely chop. With machine running, add oil in a steady stream. Add Parmesan cheese and black pepper to taste, and process to combine.

3   Spoon sauce over pasta and toss to combine. Serve immediately.

Serves 6

Coriander, a member of the carrot family, is indigenous to the Mediterranean. Also known as cilantro and Chinese parsley, it has a fresh taste and is popular in Indian, Asian, Mexican, South American and Middle Eastern cooking.

Garlic Spaghetti with Watercress

300 g/9^{1}/$_{2}$ oz spaghetti
60 g/2 oz butter
3 cloves garlic, crushed
60 g/2 oz watercress sprigs
4 tablespoons grated Parmesan cheese
freshly ground black pepper

1   Cook spaghetti in boiling water in a large saucepan following packet directions. Drain, set aside and keep warm.

2   Melt butter in a large frying pan and cook garlic, over a low heat, for 3-4 minutes. Remove pan from heat and add spaghetti, watercress and Parmesan cheese. Season to taste with black pepper and toss to combine. Serve immediately.

Serves 4

When cooking garlic it is important to use a low heat so that the garlic does not brown or burn. Burnt garlic has an unpleasant, bitter taste.

Fettuccine with Coriander Sauce

TOMATO PASTA ROLLS

2 cups/250 g/8 oz flour
2 eggs
2 tablespoons water
2 tablespoons concentrated
tomato paste (purée)
1 tablespoon olive oil

SPINACH FILLING
500 g/1 lb frozen spinach, thawed
and well drained
375 g/12 oz ricotta or
cottage cheese
2 eggs
90 g/3 oz grated Parmesan cheese
1 teaspoon ground nutmeg
freshly ground black pepper
12 slices prosciutto or thinly sliced ham
500 g/1 lb sliced mozzarella cheese

When the menu calls for finger food, and something a little more substantial is required, these rolls are ideal. Or serve individual slices with a small green salad as a colourful first course for a dinner party. Either way, the time taken to make these will be well rewarded.

1   Place flour, eggs, water, tomato paste (purée) and oil in a food processor and process to combine. Turn dough onto a lightly floured surface and knead for 5 minutes or until dough is smooth and elastic. Wrap dough in plastic food wrap and set aside to stand for 15 minutes.

2   To make filling, place spinach, ricotta cheese, eggs, Parmesan cheese, nutmeg and black pepper to taste in a bowl, and mix to combine.

3   Divide dough in half and roll out one half to form a rectangle 30 x 45 cm/12 x 18 in. Spread with half the filling mixture, leaving a 2.5 cm/1 in border, then top with half the prosciutto or ham and half the mozzarella cheese. Fold in borders on long sides, then roll up from the short side. Wrap roll in a piece of washed calico cloth and secure ends with string. Repeat with remaining ingredients to make a second roll.

4   Half fill a baking dish with water and place on the stove top. Bring to the boil, add rolls, reduce heat, cover dish with aluminium foil or lid and simmer for 30 minutes. Turn rolls once or twice during cooking. Remove rolls from water and allow to cool for 5 minutes. Remove calico from rolls and refrigerate until firm. To serve, cut rolls into slices.

Serves 12

Tomato Pasta Rolls

Spaghetti and Pesto

500 g/1 lb spaghetti

PESTO
125 g/4 oz fresh basil leaves
3 tablespoons pine nuts
4 cloves garlic, crushed
4 tablespoons olive oil
freshly ground black pepper

1   Cook spaghetti in boiling water in a large saucepan following packet directions. Drain, set aside and keep warm.

2   To make Pesto, place basil, pine nuts and garlic in a food processor or blender and process to finely chop all ingredients. With machine running, add oil in a steady steam. Season to taste with black pepper.

3   Add Pesto to spaghetti and toss to combine. Serve immediately.

Pesto is delicious served with any ribbon pasta. You might like to use fettuccine, tagliatelle or pappardelle in place of the spaghetti in this recipe. Pesto is also wonderful stirred into vegetable soups, tossed through steamed or microwaved vegetables and added to mayonnaise to make an interesting dressing for potato salad.

Spaghetti and Pesto

Serves 6

SMOKED SALMON FETTUCCINE

500 g/1 lb fettuccine

SMOKED SALMON SAUCE
125 g/4 oz fresh or frozen peas
$^1/_4$ cup/60 mL/2 fl oz white wine
$1^1/_4$ cups/315 mL/10 fl oz cream
(double)
8 slices smoked salmon
3 spring onions, finely chopped
freshly ground black pepper

1   Cook fettuccine in boiling water in a large saucepan following packet directions. Drain, set aside and keep warm.

2   To make sauce, blanch peas in boiling water for 2 minutes. Refresh under cold running water, drain and set aside. Place wine in a large frying pan and bring to the boil. Stir in 1 cup/ 250 mL/8 fl oz cream and boil until sauce reduces and thickens. Place 4 slices smoked salmon, spring onions and remaining cream in a food processor and purée. Stir smoked salmon mixture into sauce and cook until sauce is hot.

3   Cut remaining salmon slices into strips. Add salmon strips and peas to sauce and season to taste with black pepper. Spoon sauce over fettuccine and toss to combine. Serve immediately.

Smoked Salmon Fettuccine

Serves 6

CHICKEN AND LEEK ROLLS

12 spinach lasagne sheets
2 tablespoons grated fresh
Parmesan cheese

CHICKEN AND LEEK FILLING
2 teaspoons vegetable oil
3 leeks, finely sliced
3 chicken breast fillets, cut into
thin strips
$^1/_2$ cup/125 mL/4 fl oz chicken stock
3 teaspoons cornflour blended with
2 tablespoons water
1 teaspoon French mustard
2 teaspoons chopped fresh basil
freshly ground black pepper

1   Cook lasagne sheets in boiling water in a large saucepan until tender. Drain, set aside and keep warm.

2   To make filling, heat oil in a large frying pan and cook leeks and chicken, stirring, for 4-5 minutes or until chicken is brown. Stir in stock, cornflour mixture, mustard and basil and cook, stirring, for 2 minutes longer. Season to taste with black pepper.

3   Place spoonfuls of filling on lasagne sheets, roll up, top with Parmesan cheese and serve immediately.

Serves 6

Chicken and Leek Rolls

MAIN MEALS

Pasta is a food of our times. In recent years it has graduated from being a humble staple to a sought-after food. It is available in many shapes, sizes and flavours from supermarkets, corner shops … in fact almost anywhere that food is sold.

Fettuccine with Leeks

500 g/1 lb fettuccine
60 g/2 oz butter
2 large leeks, halved and thinly sliced
185 g/6 oz ham, cut into strips
1 red pepper, cut into strips
1 cup/250 mL/8 fl oz cream (double)
freshly ground black pepper

1   Cook fettuccine in boiling water in a large saucepan following packet directions. Drain, set aside and keep warm.

2   Heat butter in a large frying pan and cook leeks for 8-10 minutes or until tender. Add ham and red pepper and cook for 2-3 minutes longer. Stir in cream, bring to the boil, then reduce heat and simmer for 4-5 minutes.

3   Add fettuccine to pan and toss to combine. Serve immediately.

Serves 4

Fresh or packaged dried pasta? Which is the best? Neither is superior – they are just different. Fresh pasta is more delicate and keeps for only a few days, while dried pasta is more robust and ideal for serving with heartier sauces. Dried pasta also has the advantage of being less expensive, easier to store and of having a longer life. With a packet of pasta in the house there's a meal only minutes away.

Tuna Cannelloni

2 sheets fresh tomato lasagne
4 tablespoons grated Parmesan cheese

TUNA AND MUSHROOM FILLING
1 onion, finely sliced
1 clove garlic, crushed
125 g/4 oz mushrooms, chopped
250 g/8 oz ricotta or cottage cheese
440 g/14 oz canned tuna in water, drained and $^1/2$ cup/125 mL/4 fl oz liquid reserved
2 tablespoons finely chopped fresh dill
freshly ground black pepper

YOGURT SAUCE
15 g/$^1/2$ oz butter
2 tablespoons flour
1 teaspoon lemon juice
1 cup/200 g/6$^1/2$ oz natural yogurt
freshly ground black pepper

1   To make filling, place onion and garlic in a nonstick frying pan and cook, stirring, for 4-5 minutes or until onion is soft. Add mushrooms and cook, stirring, for 3-4 minutes longer. Place ricotta cheese and tuna in a bowl and mix to combine. Stir in mushroom mixture and dill. Season to taste with black pepper.

2   Cut lasagne sheets in half. Spoon filling down the centre of each half sheet and roll up. Place rolls join side down in a lightly oiled ovenproof dish.

3   To make sauce, melt butter in a small saucepan, stir in flour and cook for 1 minute. Stir in reserved tuna liquid and lemon juice and cook, stirring, for 3-4 minutes or until sauce thickens. Remove pan from heat and set aside to cool. Mix in yogurt and season to taste with black pepper. Return pan to a low heat and cook for 2-3 minutes longer.

4   Pour sauce over cannelloni and sprinkle with Parmesan cheese. Bake for 30 minutes or until heated through and top is golden.

Oven temperature
180°C, 350°F, Gas 4

Rather than making up the cannelloni from lasagne sheets, you may prefer to use purchased cannelloni tubes. Make up the filling as described in recipe and use to fill the tubes. Then place in an ovenproof dish, top with sauce and Parmesan cheese, and bake as directed in recipe.

Fettuccine with Leeks   *Serves 4*

SPAGHETTI WITH RATATOUILLE SAUCE

500 g/1 lb wholemeal spaghetti
4 tablespoons grated Parmesan cheese

RATATOUILLE SAUCE
1 eggplant (aubergine), diced
1 large onion, sliced
1 clove garlic, crushed
1 green pepper, diced
2 zucchini (courgettes), diced
500 g/1 lb tomatoes, peeled, seeded and
roughly chopped
$^1/_2$ cup/125 mL/4 fl oz dry white wine
1 tablespoon finely chopped fresh basil
$^1/_2$ teaspoon dried thyme
$^1/_2$ teaspoon dried oregano
freshly ground black pepper

1   To make sauce, place eggplant (aubergine), onion, garlic, green pepper, zucchini (courgettes), tomatoes, wine, basil, thyme and oregano in a nonstick frying pan, and cook over a low heat, stirring occasionally, for 30-45 minutes or until mixture forms a thick sauce. Season to taste with black pepper.

2   Cook spaghetti in boiling water in a large saucepan following packet directions. Drain spaghetti, spoon sauce over, toss to combine and sprinkle with Parmesan cheese.

Serves 4

Use this delicious and versatile Ratatouille Sauce as a topping for baked potatoes, or eat it on its own, hot or cold. The length of cooking time depends upon whether you wish the texture of the sauce to be crunchy or very soft.

SEAFOOD FETTUCCINE

500 g/1 lb mixed coloured fettuccine

SPICY SEAFOOD SAUCE
1 tablespoon olive oil
1 onion, sliced
1 red pepper, diced
1 clove garlic, crushed
1 red chilli, seeded and finely chopped
$^1/_2$ teaspoon ground cumin
$^1/_2$ teaspoon ground coriander
440 g/14 oz canned tomatoes,
undrained and mashed
$^1/_4$ cup/60 mL/2 fl oz dry white wine
1 tablespoon tomato paste (purée)
155 g/5 oz calamari, cut into rings
155 g/5 oz cleaned fresh mussels
in shells
500 g/1 lb uncooked large prawns,
peeled and deveined
4 tablespoons finely chopped
fresh coriander
freshly ground black pepper

1   To make sauce, heat oil in a large saucepan and cook onion, red pepper, garlic, chilli, cumin and ground coriander for 3-4 minutes or until onion is soft. Add tomatoes, wine and tomato paste (purée) and cook over a medium heat for 30 minutes longer or until sauce reduces and thickens.

2   Add calamari to sauce and cook for 5 minutes or until just tender. Add mussels and prawns and cook for 4-5 minutes longer. Mix in 2 tablespoons fresh coriander. Season to taste with black pepper.

3   Cook fettuccine in boiling water in a large saucepan following packet directions. Drain, then spoon sauce over fettuccine and sprinkle with remaining fresh coriander. Serve immediately.

Serves 4

Accompany this simple, spicy meal with a salad made of your favourite vegetables. You might like to try a salad of raw spinach, orange segments, thinly sliced mushrooms and spring onions, tossed in a light vinaigrette dressing.

Spaghetti with Ratatouille Sauce,
Tuna Cannelloni, Seafood Fettuccine

PENNE, BACON AND BASIL

500 g/1 lb penne
1 tablespoon olive oil
2 cloves garlic, crushed
6 rashers bacon, chopped
2 tablespoons chopped fresh basil
60 g/2 oz chopped walnuts
freshly ground black pepper
30 g/1 oz grated Parmesan cheese

1   Cook penne in boiling water in a large saucepan following packet directions. Drain, set aside and keep warm.

2   Heat oil in a large frying pan and cook garlic over a medium heat for 1 minute. Add bacon and cook for 2-3 minutes longer or until bacon is crispy. Add basil, walnuts and penne to pan, season to taste with black pepper and toss to combine. Sprinkle with Parmesan cheese and serve immediately.

Penne. Bacon and Basil
Ravioli with Vegetable Medley

Serves 4

RAVIOLI WITH VEGETABLE MEDLEY

500 g/1 lb ravioli of your choice
30 g/1 oz butter
2 cloves garlic, crushed
125 g/4 oz button mushrooms, halved
125 g/4 oz green beans, cut into
1 cm/^{1}/$_2$ in lengths
125 g/4 oz cherry tomatoes, quartered
freshly ground black pepper
30 g/1 oz grated Parmesan cheese

1   Cook ravioli in boiling water in a large saucepan following packet directions. Drain, set aside and keep warm.

2   Melt butter in a large frying pan and cook garlic and mushrooms for 2-3 minutes. Add beans and tomatoes, season to taste with black pepper and cook for 2 minutes longer.

3   Add ravioli and Parmesan cheese to pan and toss to combine. Serve immediately.

Serves 4

The microwave oven has made reheating pasta not only easy but successful in a way that it never was before. To reheat pasta in the microwave, place cooked pasta, with or without sauce, in a covered, microwave-safe dish and reheat on HIGH (100%), stirring once or twice, for 2-3 minutes, or until pasta is hot. The exact length of time will of course depend on how much pasta you are reheating.

PORK PIE

375 g/12 oz prepared shortcrust pastry
60 g/2 oz grated tasty cheese
(mature Cheddar)

PORK AND MUSHROOM FILLING
30 g/1 oz butter
1 onion, chopped
500 g/1 lb lean pork mince
1 cup/250 g/8 oz tomato purée
^{1}/$_2$ cup/125 mL/4 fl oz dry white wine
250 g/8 oz button mushrooms, sliced

MACARONI FILLING
185 g/6 oz macaroni
30 g/1 oz butter
2 tablespoons flour
1 cup/250 mL/8 fl oz hot milk
1 tablespoon chopped fresh parsley
freshly ground black pepper

1   Roll out pastry to fit a deep-sided 23 cm/9 in flan dish. Line pastry case with nonstick baking paper and weigh down with uncooked rice. Bake pastry case for 10-15 minutes, then remove rice and paper and set pastry case aside to cool.

2   To make Pork and Mushroom Filling, melt butter in a large saucepan and cook onion for 2-3 minutes, then add pork and cook, stirring to break up meat, for 10 minutes longer or until meat changes colour. Stir in tomato purée, wine and mushrooms. Bring meat mixture to simmering and simmer for 20 minutes.

3   To make Macaroni Filling, cook macaroni in boiling water in a large saucepan following packet directions. Drain and set aside. Melt butter in a saucepan over a medium heat, then stir in flour and cook for 1 minute. Stir in hot milk and cook, stirring constantly, for 4-5 minutes or until sauce thickens. Remove sauce from heat and stir in macaroni and parsley. Season to taste with black pepper.

4   Spread Pork and Mushroom Filling over base of pastry case, top with Macaroni Filling and sprinkle with cheese. Reduce oven temperature to 180°C/350°F/Gas 4 and bake pie for 25-30 minutes or until top is golden.

Serves 6

Oven temperature
200°C, 400°F, Gas 6

Pasta is a complex carbohydrate which means that it sustains and releases energy over a long period of time and so is a favoured food of athletes and others with high energy demands. Pasta itself is low in fat and calories; it's the sauce and other ingredients that you add that can do the damage. So, if you are watching the calories, choose sauces that are low in fat. Fresh vegetable sauces without cream and fresh tomato sauces are good choices. Remember to top pasta dishes with only a little cheese.

Below: Pork Pie
Below right: Red Pepper, Cheese and Fettuccine

Red Pepper, Cheese and Fettuccine

500 g/1 lb fettuccine
2 tablespoons oil
2 cloves garlic, crushed
2 red peppers, cut into strips
8 spring onions, cut into thin strips
1 teaspoon cracked black pepper
90 g/3 oz goat's cheese, crumbled

1 Cook fettuccine in boiling water in a large saucepan following packet directions. Drain, set aside and keep warm.

2 Heat oil in a large frying pan and cook garlic and red peppers for 2 minutes. Add spring onions and black pepper and cook for 1 minute longer. Add fettuccine and cheese to red pepper mixture and toss to combine. Serve immediately.

Serves 4

When buying goat's cheese, the colour of the cheese under the rind should be chalk-white. The cheese should be fresh and tangy, with no smell of ammonia.

Bean Lasagne

BEAN LASAGNE

Oven temperature
180°C, 350°F, Gas 4

12 spinach leaves, chopped
250 g/8 oz lasagne sheets
125 g/4 oz grated tasty cheese
(mature Cheddar)
2 tablespoons grated Parmesan cheese

TOMATO BEAN SAUCE
1 tablespoon olive oil
2 onions, chopped
2 cloves garlic, crushed
440 g/14 oz canned tomatoes, undrained
440 g/14 oz canned lima or butter beans,
drained and puréed
440 g/14 oz canned red kidney beans,
drained
1 teaspoon hot chilli sauce
1 teaspoon dried oregano

Serves 6

1   To make sauce, heat oil in a large frying pan and cook onions and garlic for 4-5 minutes or until onions are soft. Stir in tomatoes, lima, or butter, bean purée, red kidney beans, chilli sauce and oregano. Bring to the boil, then reduce heat and simmer, uncovered, for 10 minutes or until sauce reduces and thickens. Remove sauce from heat and set aside.

2   Place a little water in a saucepan and bring to the boil, add spinach and cook for 1-2 minutes or until spinach wilts. Drain and set aside. Cook lasagne sheets in boiling water in a large saucepan following packet directions. Drain.

3   Place one-third lasagne sheets in the base of a lightly greased, shallow ovenproof dish, then top with one-third of the bean sauce and half of the spinach. Repeat layers, then finish with a layer of lasagne sheets and remaining bean sauce. Sprinkle with tasty cheese (mature Cheddar) and Parmesan cheese. Bake for 30 minutes or until lasagne is heated through and top is golden.

Quick Fettuccine with Scallops

500 g/1 lb fettuccine
1 tablespoon finely chopped
fresh parsley

SCALLOP SAUCE
30 g/1 oz butter
1 red pepper, cut into strips
2 spring onions, finely chopped
1 cup/250 mL/8 fl oz cream (double)
500 g/1 lb scallops
freshly ground black pepper

1   Cook fettuccine in boiling water in a large saucepan following packet directions. Drain, set aside and keep warm.

2   To make sauce, melt butter in a large frying pan and cook red pepper and spring onions for 1-2 minutes. Add cream and bring to the boil, then reduce heat and simmer for 5 minutes or until sauce reduces slightly and thickens.

3   Stir scallops into sauce and cook for 2-3 minutes or until scallops are opaque. Season to taste with black pepper. Place fettuccine in a warm serving bowl, top with sauce and sprinkle with parsley.

Serves 4

A salad of mixed lettuces refreshes the palate and is the ideal accompaniment for this rich dish.

Quick Fettuccine with Scallops

SPAGHETTI WITH ASPARAGUS

500 g/1 lb wholemeal spaghetti
60 g/2 oz grated Parmesan cheese

ASPARAGUS SAUCE
1 tablespoon olive oil
1 clove garlic, crushed
440 g/14 oz canned tomatoes,
drained and chopped
315 g/10 oz canned
asparagus cuts (tips), drained
1 tablespoon chopped fresh parsley
1 tablespoon brown sugar
2 tablespoons red wine
freshly ground black pepper

1 Cook spaghetti in boiling water in a large saucepan following packet directions. Drain, set aside and keep warm.

2 To make sauce, heat oil in a frying pan and cook garlic over a medium heat for 1 minute. Stir in tomatoes, asparagus, parsley, sugar and wine. Bring to simmering, cover and simmer for 15-20 minutes or until sauce reduces and thickens. Season to taste with black pepper. Spoon sauce over spaghetti and top with Parmesan cheese. Serve immediately.

Spaghetti with Asparagus,
Tuna Lasagne

Serves 4

Tuna Lasagne

15 g/^{1}/$_2$ oz butter
2 stalks celery, finely chopped
1 onion, chopped
9 sheets instant (no precooking
required) lasagne
440 g/14 oz canned tuna, drained
and flaked
2 tablespoons grated tasty cheese
(mature Cheddar)
1 teaspoon curry powder
^{1}/$_2$ teaspoon ground paprika

CURRY SAUCE
2 cups/500 mL/16 fl oz milk
1 cup/250 mL/8 fl oz water
30 g/1 oz butter
^{1}/$_3$ cup/45 g/1^1/$_2$ oz flour
2 teaspoons curry powder
2 eggs, beaten
2 tablespoons grated tasty cheese
(mature Cheddar)
freshly ground black pepper

Serves 6

1 To make sauce, combine milk and water and set aside. Melt butter in a saucepan, stir in flour and curry powder and cook for 2-3 minutes. Remove pan from heat and whisk in milk mixture. Return sauce to heat and cook, stirring constantly, for 4-5 minutes or until sauce boils and thickens. Remove pan from heat and whisk in eggs and cheese. Season to taste with black pepper.

2 Melt butter in a frying pan and cook celery and onion for 4-5 minutes or until onion is soft. Spoon a little sauce over the base of a lightly greased shallow ovenproof dish. Top with three lasagne sheets and spread over half the tuna and half the celery mixture, then a layer of sauce. Repeat layers, finishing with a layer of lasagne, then sauce.

3 Combine cheese, curry powder and paprika, and sprinkle over lasagne. Bake for 30-35 minutes or until noodles are tender and top is golden.

Oven temperature
190°C, 375°F, Gas 5

This recipe freezes well. Thaw overnight in the refrigerator before reheating at 180°C, 350°F, Gas 4 for 30 minutes.

Pasta with Artichokes

375 g/12 oz spiral pasta
2 tablespoons Parmesan cheese

ARTICHOKE SAUCE
1 tablespoon olive oil
1 onion, chopped
2 cloves garlic, crushed
4 large ripe tomatoes, peeled
and chopped
2 tablespoons chopped fresh basil
2 tablespoons chopped fresh parsley
440 g/14 oz canned artichoke hearts,
drained and halved
freshly ground black pepper

1 To make sauce, heat oil in a saucepan and cook onion and garlic over a medium heat until onion is soft. Stir in tomatoes, basil and parsley and bring to the boil. Reduce heat, cover and simmer, stirring occasionally, for 30 minutes or until sauce reduces and thickens. Stir in artichokes and season to taste with black pepper.

2 Cook pasta in boiling water in a large saucepan following packet directions. Drain, spoon sauce over hot pasta, sprinkle with Parmesan cheese and serve immediately.

Serves 4

The globe artichoke is one of the most popular vegetables in Italy. It is actually a cultivated thistle grown for its edible, immature flower heads.
In this sauce the hard work has been taken out of preparing the artichokes by using canned ones.

MUSHROOM BOLOGNESE

500 g/1 lb spaghetti

BOLOGNESE SAUCE
2 tablespoons olive oil
220 g/7 oz mushrooms, sliced
1 carrot, finely chopped
1 onion, finely chopped
1 clove garlic, crushed
$^1/_2$ teaspoon chilli powder
500 g/1 lb lean beef mince
155 g/5 oz prosciutto or bacon,
finely chopped
ground nutmeg
$^3/_4$ cup/185 mL/6 fl oz dry red wine
$^1/_2$ cup/125 g/4 oz tomato paste (purée)
440 g/14 oz canned tomatoes,
undrained and mashed
$^1/_2$ cup/125 mL/4 fl oz water
freshly ground black pepper

You may wish to accompany this delicious main meal with freshly grated Parmesan cheese, a green salad and crusty bread.

1 To make sauce, heat oil in a large frying pan and cook mushrooms, carrot and onion for 4-5 minutes or until onion is soft. Stir in garlic and chilli powder and cook for 1 minute longer.

2 Add beef and prosciutto or bacon to pan and cook over a medium heat, stirring to break up meat, for 4-5 minutes or until meat changes colour. Drain off any fat and season to taste with nutmeg.

3 Stir wine, tomato paste (purée), tomatoes and water into pan. Bring to the boil, then reduce heat and simmer, stirring occasionally, for 30 minutes or until sauce reduces and thickens. Season to taste with black pepper.

4 Cook spaghetti in boiling water in a large saucepan following packet directions. Drain, place in warmed serving bowls, top with sauce and serve immediately.

Serves 6

Mushroom Bolognese

SPRING TAGLIATELLE

Spring Tagliatelle

250 g/8 oz cauliflower florets
250 g/8 oz broccoli florets
250 g/8 oz tagliatelle
4 tablespoons olive oil
2 cloves garlic, crushed
1 small eggplant (aubergine),
cut into strips
$^1/_2$ red pepper, cut into strips
$^1/_2$ green pepper, cut into strips
2 tablespoons chopped fresh basil
freshly ground black pepper
30 g/1 oz grated fresh Parmesan cheese

1   Blanch cauliflower and broccoli in boiling water for 1 minute or cook in microwave for 1 minute. Drain and refresh under cold running water, drain again and set aside.

2   Cook tagliatelle in boiling water in a large saucepan following packet directions. Drain, set aside and keep warm.

3   Heat oil in a large frying pan and cook garlic and eggplant (aubergine), red pepper and green pepper over a medium heat for 4-5 minutes. Add tagliatelle, cauliflower, broccoli and basil to pan and toss to combine. Season to taste with black pepper and sprinkle with Parmesan cheese. Serve immediately.

Serves 4

This medley of lightly cooked vegetables, fresh basil and pasta makes a delectable combination. To complete the meal, serve with crusty bread and a salad of mixed lettuce and fresh herbs tossed in a garlicky dressing.

Cheesy Meatballs with Spaghetti

CHEESY MEATBALLS WITH SPAGHETTI

250 g/8 oz spaghetti

CHEESY MEATBALLS
500 g/1 lb lean beef mince
2 tablespoons finely chopped
fresh parsley
$^1/_2$ cup/60 g/2 oz grated Parmesan cheese
2 teaspoons tomato paste (purée)
1 egg, beaten

TOMATO SAUCE
15 g/$^1/_2$ oz butter
1 onion, finely chopped
2 teaspoons dried basil
1 teaspoon dried oregano
440 g/14 oz canned tomatoes,
undrained and mashed
2 tablespoons tomato paste (purée)
$^1/_2$ cup/125 mL/4 fl oz beef stock
$^1/_2$ cup/125 mL/4 fl oz white wine
1 teaspoon caster sugar
freshly ground black pepper

What's the easiest way to eat ribbon pasta? Firstly, serve it in a shallow bowl or on a plate with a slight rim. To ensure that the pasta stays hot while you are eating it, heat the plates before serving. To eat the pasta, slip a few strands on to your fork, then twirl them against the plate, or a spoon, into a ball – the trick is to take only small forkfuls and to wind the pasta tightly so that there are no dangling strands.

1 To make meatballs, place beef, parsley, Parmesan cheese, tomato paste (purée) and egg in a bowl, and mix to combine. Form mixture into small balls and cook in a nonstick frying pan for 4-5 minutes or until brown. Remove meatballs from pan and drain on absorbent kitchen paper.

2 To make sauce, melt butter in a large frying pan and cook onion, basil and oregano for 2-3 minutes or until onion is soft. Stir in tomatoes, tomato paste (purée), beef stock, wine and sugar. Bring to the boil, then reduce heat and simmer, stirring occasionally, for 30 minutes or until sauce reduces and thickens. Season to taste with black pepper. Add meatballs to sauce and cook for 5 minutes longer.

3 Cook spaghetti in boiling water in a large saucepan following packet directions. Drain, place in a warm serving bowl and top with meatballs and sauce. Serve immediately.

Serves 4

CHICKEN, PASTA TOSS

500 g/1 lb shell pasta
30 g/1 oz butter
1 onion, finely chopped
1 clove garlic, crushed
250 g/8 oz cooked chicken, shredded
1/2 cup/125 mL/4 fl oz chicken stock
6 spinach leaves, shredded
freshly ground black pepper
60 g/2 oz pine nuts, toasted

1 Cook pasta in boiling water in a large saucepan following packet directions. Drain, set aside and keep warm.

2 Melt butter in a large frying pan and cook onion and garlic, stirring, over a medium heat for 3-4 minutes. Add chicken and stock, and cook for 4-5 minutes longer.

3 Add spinach and pasta to pan, season to taste with black pepper and toss to combine. Sprinkle with pine nuts and serve immediately.

Serves 4

Chicken, Pasta Toss

This pretty pasta dish looks wonderful served with a salad of julienne carrots. To make the salad, cut 3 large carrots into strips and boil or microwave until just tender. Drain, refresh under cold running water, drain again and place in a salad bowl. Place 2 tablespoons lemon juice, 1 tablespoon Dijon mustard, 4 tablespoons olive oil and 1 tablespoon snipped fresh chives in a screwtop jar and shake to combine. Spoon over carrots and toss to combine. Cover and chill for 1 hour or until required.

BEEF LASAGNE

Oven temperature
190°C, 375°F, Gas 5

6 sheets instant (no precooking required)
lasagne
60 g/2 oz grated tasty cheese
(mature Cheddar)
2 tablespoons grated Parmesan cheese

MEAT SAUCE
2 teaspoons olive oil
1 onion, chopped
2 cloves garlic, crushed
2 rashers bacon, chopped
125 g/4 oz button mushrooms, sliced
500 g/1 lb lean beef mince
440 g/14 oz canned tomatoes,
undrained and mashed
$^1/_2$ cup/125 mL/4 fl oz red wine
$^1/_2$ teaspoon dried basil
$^1/_2$ teaspoon dried oregano
1 teaspoon sugar

SPINACH CHEESE SAUCE
30 g/1oz butter
2 tablespoons flour
1 cup/250 mL/8 fl oz milk
$^1/_2$ cup/125 mL/4 fl oz cream (single)
$^1/_2$ cup/60 g/2 oz grated tasty cheese
(mature Cheddar)
250 g/8 oz frozen spinach, thawed
and drained
freshly ground black pepper

1   To make Meat Sauce, heat oil in a
large frying pan and cook, onion, garlic,
bacon and mushrooms over a medium
heat for 4-5 minutes or until onion is
soft.

2   Add beef to pan and cook, stirring to
break up meat, for 4-5 minutes or until
meat is brown. Combine tomatoes, wine,
basil, oregano and sugar, and pour into
pan with meat mixture. Bring to the boil,
then reduce heat, cover and simmer for
35 minutes or until sauce thickens.

3   To make Spinach Cheese Sauce,
melt butter in a saucepan and cook flour
for 1-2 minutes. Remove pan from heat
and stir in milk and cream. Cook,
stirring constantly, over a medium heat
for 4-5 minutes or until sauce boils and
thickens. Remove pan from heat and stir
in cheese and spinach. Season to taste
with black pepper.

4   To assemble lasagne, spread one-third
of the Spinach Cheese Sauce over base
of a lightly greased, shallow 28 x 18 cm/
11 x 7 in ovenproof dish. Top with three
lasagne sheets, spread half the Meat
Sauce over, then another third of the
Spinach Cheese Sauce. Top with
another three lasagne sheets and
remaining Meat Sauce. Place remaining
lasagne sheets over Meat Sauce and top
with remaining Spinach Cheese Sauce.

5   Combine tasty cheese (mature
Cheddar) and Parmesan cheese and
sprinkle over lasagne and bake for 40
minutes or until top is golden.

Serves 6

As an accompaniment to
this substantial lasagne
choose something light, such
as a tomato and herb salad.

Right: Beef Lasagne

TORTELLINI WITH RED PEPPER SAUCE

500 g/1 lb tortellini

RED PEPPER SAUCE
1 tablespoon vegetable oil
1 onion, chopped
440 g/14 oz canned sweet red peppers,
drained and chopped
1 cup/250 mL/8 fl oz water
1 tablespoon honey
1 tablespoon chopped fresh oregano
freshly ground black pepper

1   Cook tortellini in boiling water in a large saucepan, following packet directions. Drain, set aside and keep warm.

2   To make sauce, heat oil in a small frying pan and cook onion, stirring, for 3 minutes or until onion is soft. Place red peppers, water, honey, oregano and onion in a food processor or blender and process to make a smooth sauce.

3   Pour pepper sauce into a large saucepan and heat over a medium heat for 4-5 minutes or until sauce is simmering. Season to taste with black pepper. Spoon sauce over tortellini and toss to combine.

Serves 4

Canned sweet red peppers are available from Continental delicatessens and some supermarkets. They are sometimes called pimentos.
You may wish to use fresh red peppers instead of the canned ones. You will require 4 large peppers for this recipe and they need to be roasted and the skin removed before making the sauce.

SAUCES

Nothing beats a bowl of perfectly cooked pasta topped with a delicious sauce and sprinkled with freshly grated Parmesan cheese. These sauces make pasta into something special and are sure to be popular.

Creamy Pumpkin
Sauce

Yogurt Herb Sauce

Chicken Liver Sauce

Tomato Sauce

Tomato Bolognese
Sauce

Ravioli with Tuna
Sauce

Asparagus Sauce

Mushroom Pasta
Sauce

Yogurt Herb Sauce

CREAMY PUMPKIN SAUCE

500 g/1 lb fettuccine

PUMPKIN SAUCE
250 g/8 oz pumpkin, cut into strips
2 cups/500 mL/16 fl oz cream (double)
125 g/4 oz pumpkin, cooked and mashed
$^1/_2$ teaspoon ground nutmeg
freshly ground black pepper
1 teaspoon snipped fresh chives

1   Cook fettuccine in boiling water in a large saucepan following packet directions. Drain, set aside and keep warm.

2   To make sauce, boil, steam or microwave pumpkin strips until just tender. Drain, refresh under cold running water and set aside.

3   Place cream in a large frying pan and bring to the boil. Reduce heat and simmer for 10-15 minutes or until cream is reduced by half. Whisk mashed pumpkin, nutmeg and black pepper to taste into cream and cook for 2-3 minutes longer. Then stir pumpkin strips and chives into sauce and cook for 2-3 minutes.

4   Spoon sauce over fettuccine and toss to combine. Serve immediately.

Serves 4

The people of Mantua in northern Italy have a reputation for being pumpkin eaters. This pretty pasta sauce would, no doubt, be much to their liking. Pumpkins, tomatoes, red and green peppers, beans and corn are all vegetables of the New World. They arrived in Italy during the sixteenth century.

YOGURT HERB SAUCE

500 g/1 lb mixed coloured spiral pasta

YOGURT HERB SAUCE
15 g/$^1/_2$ oz butter
1 small onion, chopped
1 clove garlic, crushed
2 tablespoons flour
$^1/_2$ cup/125 mL/4 fl oz vegetable stock
1 cup/200 g/6$^1/_2$ oz natural yogurt
2 tablespoons finely chopped
fresh parsley
2 tablespoons finely chopped fresh basil
2 tablespoons snipped fresh chives
freshly ground black pepper

1   Cook pasta in boiling water in a large saucepan following packet directions. Drain, set aside and keep warm.

2   To make sauce, melt butter in a saucepan and cook onion and garlic over a medium heat for 2-3 minutes. Stir in flour and stock and cook, stirring constantly, for 4-5 minutes longer or until sauce boils and thickens.

3   Remove pan from heat, stir in yogurt and cook over a low heat for 2-3 minutes longer. Mix in parsley, basil and chives and season to taste with black pepper. Spoon sauce over pasta and serve immediately.

Serves 4

This tasty low-kilojoule (calorie) sauce is also great spooned over steamed vegetables. If watching the kilojoules (calories) it makes an original alternative to white sauce. You may wish to use low-fat yogurt to further reduce fat and kilojoule (calorie) content.

CHICKEN LIVER SAUCE

30 g/1 oz butter
4 rashers bacon, chopped
1 onion, finely chopped
1 clove garlic, crushed
375 g/12 oz chicken livers, chopped
2 teaspoons flour
$^3/_4$ cup/185 mL/6 fl oz chicken stock
1 teaspoon tomato paste (purée)
1 teaspoon chopped fresh marjoram or
$^1/_2$ teaspoon dried marjoram
freshly ground black pepper
$^1/_4$ cup/60 g/2 oz sour cream

Serves 4

To serve, spoon sauce over pasta and garnish with fresh marjoram sprigs if desired. This sauce goes well with pastas such as rigatoni, penne and farfelle.

1   Melt butter in a saucepan and cook bacon, onion and garlic over a medium heat for 4-5 minutes or until onion is soft. Add chicken livers and cook, stirring, for 4-5 minutes or until livers change colour.

2   Stir in flour, then gradually blend in stock. Add tomato paste (purée), marjoram and black pepper to taste. Cover and cook, stirring occasionally, over a low heat for 10 minutes. Just prior to serving, stir in sour cream.

TOMATO SAUCE

1 tablespoon olive oil
1 onion, finely chopped
1 clove garlic, crushed
500 g/1 lb tomatoes, peeled and
roughly chopped
1 tablespoon tomato paste (purée)
$^1/_2$ teaspoon sugar
1 tablespoon chopped fresh basil
freshly ground black pepper

Serves 4

To serve, spoon sauce over pasta and toss to combine. Top with grated fresh Parmesan cheese and serve immediately.
This sauce is delicious with any kind of pasta.

1   Heat oil in a saucepan and cook onion and garlic over a medium heat for 4-5 minutes or until onion is soft. Add tomatoes, tomato paste (purée), sugar and basil.

2   Bring sauce to simmering, cover and simmer, stirring occasionally, for 30 minutes or until sauce reduces and thickens. Season to taste with black pepper.

TOMATO BOLOGNESE SAUCE

2 tablespoons olive oil
2 rashers bacon, chopped
1 onion, chopped
1 carrot, chopped
1 stalk celery, chopped
1 clove garlic, crushed
250 g/8 oz lean beef mince
125 g/4 oz chicken livers, chopped
2 tablespoons tomato paste (purée)
$^1/_2$ cup/125 mL/4 fl oz dry white wine
$^1/_2$ cup/125 mL/4 fl oz beef or
chicken stock
pinch ground nutmeg
freshly ground black pepper

1   Heat oil in a large saucepan and cook bacon, stirring, over a medium heat for 3-4 minutes. Add onion, carrot, celery and garlic and cook, stirring, for 5 minutes longer or until vegetables start to brown.

2   Add beef mince to pan and cook, stirring to break up meat, for 5-6 minutes or until beef mince browns. Add chicken livers and cook for 2-3 minutes or until livers change colour.

3   Stir in tomato paste (purée), wine, stock and nutmeg. Bring sauce to simmering, cover and simmer for 30-40 minutes or until sauce reduces and thickens. Season to taste with black pepper.

Serves 4

To serve, spoon sauce over hot spaghetti and garnish with celery leaves if desired. This tomato-flavoured meat sauce is also excellent served with penne, macaroni, farfelle and rigatoni.

From top: Chicken Liver Sauce, Tomato Sauce,
Tomato Bolognese Sauce

RAVIOLI WITH TUNA SAUCE

375 g/12 oz fresh or frozen
spinach ravioli
2 tablespoons grated Parmesan cheese

TUNA TOMATO SAUCE
1 teaspoon olive oil
1 onion, finely chopped
1 clove garlic, crushed
440 g/14 oz canned tomatoes,
undrained and mashed
1 tablespoon tomato paste (purée)
1 tablespoon dry red wine
1 teaspoon sugar
440 g/14 oz canned tuna, drained
and flaked
1 tablespoon finely chopped fresh parsley
1 tablespoon finely chopped fresh dill
freshly ground black pepper

1 Cook ravioli in boiling water in a large saucepan following packet directions. Drain, set aside and keep warm.

2 To make sauce, heat oil in a frying pan and cook onion and garlic over a medium heat for 4-5 minutes or until onion is soft. Stir in tomatoes, tomato paste (purée), wine and sugar. Bring to the boil, then add tuna, parsley and dill. Reduce heat and simmer for 10 minutes or until sauce reduces and thickens.

3 Place ravioli on a warmed serving platter, spoon sauce over, sprinkle with Parmesan cheese and serve immediately.

Serves 4

Don't keep this tuna sauce just for ravioli; try it spooned over penne, farfelle and conchigliette.

*Ravioli with Tuna Sauce,
Asparagus Sauce*

ASPARAGUS SAUCE

500 g/1 lb spaghetti
2 tablespoons grated Parmesan cheese

ASPARAGUS SAUCE
500 g/1 lb fresh asparagus spears,
trimmed
1 tablespoon olive oil
1 thick slice wholegrain bread, crumbed
1 cup/250 mL/8 fl oz evaporated
skim milk
60 g/2 oz grated mozzarella cheese
freshly ground black pepper

Serves 6

1 Cook spaghetti in boiling water in a large saucepan following packet directions. Drain, set aside and keep warm.

2 To make sauce, steam, boil or microwave asparagus until tender. Drain and refresh under cold running water. Cut asparagus into 2.5 cm/1 in pieces and set aside.

3 Heat oil in a frying pan and cook bread crumbs over a low heat, stirring constantly, for 2 minutes. Stir in milk and asparagus, and cook, stirring occasionally, over a medium heat for 5 minutes. Mix in cheese and season to taste with black pepper.

4 Place spaghetti on a warmed serving platter, spoon sauce over and toss gently to combine. Sprinkle with Parmesan cheese and serve immediately.

Nothing beats the taste of fresh asparagus. This is a wonderful way to use fresh asparagus in season while still retaining its delicate flavour.

MUSHROOM PASTA SAUCE

375 g/12 oz fettuccine
2 tablespoons grated Parmesan cheese

MUSHROOM TOMATO SAUCE
60 g/2 oz butter
2 onions, chopped
440 g/14 oz canned tomatoes, undrained
and mashed
2 tablespoons tomato paste (purée)
125 g/4 oz mushrooms, sliced
4 zucchini (courgettes), sliced
1 tablespoon chopped fresh oregano or
1 teaspoon dried oregano
2 bay leaves
freshly ground black pepper

Serves 4

1 To make sauce, melt butter in a saucepan and cook onions for 3-4 minutes or until soft. Add tomatoes, tomato paste (purée), mushrooms, zucchini (courgettes), oregano and bay leaves and bring to the boil. Reduce heat, cover and simmer, stirring occasionally, for 30 minutes or until sauce reduces and thickens. Season to taste with black pepper.

2 Cook fettuccine in boiling water in a large saucepan following packet directions. Drain, then spoon sauce over fettuccine, sprinkle with Parmesan cheese and serve immediately.

Tomatoes, mushrooms, onions and zucchini (courgettes) combine to make a substantial vegetable sauce that is good with any type of pasta.

LIGHT MEALS

Pasta comes into its own as a fast food. These recipes take next to no time to prepare. In fact, many take less time to prepare and cook than many prepared convenience foods – and they taste wonderful.

Fettuccine with Green Sauce

375 g/12 oz fresh fettuccine

GREEN SAUCE
250 g/8 oz spinach, shredded
45 g/1^1/$_2$ oz butter
2 cloves garlic, crushed
1^1/$_2$ cups/375 mL/12 fl oz
cream (double)
125 g/4 oz grated fresh Parmesan cheese
freshly ground black pepper

1   Cook fettuccine in boiling water in a large saucepan following packet directions. Drain, set aside and keep warm.

2   To make sauce, boil, steam or microwave spinach for 2-3 minutes or until just cooked. Drain and set aside. Melt butter in a saucepan and cook garlic over a low heat for 2 minutes. Stir in cream and Parmesan cheese and cook, stirring constantly, for 2-3 minutes or until smooth. Stir spinach into sauce and season to taste with black pepper. Spoon sauce over fettuccine and toss to combine.

Serves 4

Fresh Parmesan cheese is available from continental delicatessens and some supermarkets. It is best purchased in a piece then grated as required. Once you have tried fresh Parmesan you will realise that it has a much milder and better flavour than the grated powder that comes in packets. If a recipe calls for fresh Parmesan cheese and it is unavailable, use about a third of the quantity of the packaged variety. If used in a sauce, you will notice it has a more grainy texture than fresh Parmesan.

Macaroni with Prosciutto

375 g/12 oz macaroni
45 g/1^1/$_2$ oz butter
2 cloves garlic, crushed
125 g/4 oz prosciutto or bacon,
cut into strips
6 sun-dried tomatoes, drained and
cut into strips
3 tablespoons chopped fresh basil
freshly ground black pepper

1   Cook macaroni in boiling water in a large saucepan following packet directions. Drain, set aside and keep warm.

2   Melt butter in a large saucepan and cook garlic and prosciutto or bacon over a medium heat for 5 minutes. Add tomatoes and basil and cook for 2 minutes longer.

3   Add prosciutto mixture to macaroni, season to taste with black pepper, and toss to combine. Serve immediately.

Serves 4

Prosciutto is an unsmoked, salted, air-cured ham. It is used in cooked dishes, or thinly sliced and served as part of an antipasto platter. It is also popular wrapped around melon and served as a starter.

Fettuccine with Green Sauce,
Macaroni with Proscuitto

ORIENTAL NOODLES AND VEGETABLES

500 g/1 lb Oriental noodles
1 tablespoon peanut oil
2 teaspoons grated fresh ginger
1 clove garlic, crushed
1 onion, sliced
1 carrot, sliced diagonally
2 stalks celery, sliced diagonally
90 g/3 oz bean sprouts
185 g/6 oz snow peas (mangetout),
trimmed
freshly ground black pepper

1   Cook noodles in boiling water in a large saucepan for 5-6 minutes or until cooked. Drain and set aside.

2   Heat oil in a wok or a large frying pan and stir-fry ginger and garlic for 1-2 minutes. Add onion and carrot and stir-fry for 4-5 minutes longer.

3   Toss in celery, bean sprouts and snow peas (mangetout) and cook for 2-3 minutes.

4   Stir in noodles and cook for 3-4 minutes or until noodles are heated. Season to taste with black pepper and serve immediately.

Serves 6

The flat Oriental noodles that have been used in this recipe are different from egg noodles; they are made from flour and water and are available from Chinese food stores.

TAGLIATELLE SALAD

250 g/8 oz fresh spinach tagliatelle
250 g/8 oz fresh plain tagliatelle
2 zucchini (courgettes),
cut into matchsticks
1 small red pepper, sliced
1 small green pepper, sliced
220 g/7 oz green beans, cooked

TOMATO AND BASIL DRESSING
4 ripe tomatoes, peeled and
roughly chopped
1 clove garlic, crushed
2 teaspoons olive oil
2 teaspoons red wine vinegar
2 tablespoons finely chopped fresh basil
1 tablespoon finely chopped fresh parsley
1 tablespoon snipped fresh chives
freshly ground black pepper

1   Cook both tagliatelles in boiling water in a large saucepan following packet directions. Rinse under cold running water, drain and set aside to cool completely.

2   Place cold tagliatelles, zucchini (courgettes), red and green peppers and beans in a large salad bowl.

3   To make dressing, place tomatoes, garlic, oil and vinegar in a food processor or blender and process until smooth. Stir in basil, parsley and chives and season to taste with black pepper. Spoon dressing over pasta and vegetables. Toss lightly to coat all ingredients with dressing.

Serves 6

As a luncheon, this salad tossed in a tomato and basil dressing needs only to be accompanied by crusty bread.

CREAMY MUSHROOMS AND PASTA

375 g/12 oz macaroni
3 tablespoons finely chopped
fresh parsley
2 tablespoons grated Parmesan cheese

CREAMY MUSHROOM SAUCE
2 teaspoons vegetable oil
1 onion, sliced
500 g/1 lb mushrooms, sliced
1 teaspoon paprika
2 tablespoons tomato paste (purée)
1 cup/250 mL/8 fl oz evaporated
skim milk
freshly ground black pepper

1   Cook macaroni in boiling water in a large saucepan following packet directions. Drain, set aside and keep warm.

2   To make sauce, heat oil in a large frying pan and cook onion and mushrooms for 5 minutes. Place paprika, tomato paste (purée) and milk in a bowl and whisk to combine. Stir into mushroom mixture and cook, stirring, over a low heat for 5 minutes. Season to taste with black pepper.

3   Place pasta in a heated serving dish and spoon sauce over. Toss to combine and sprinkle with parsley and Parmesan cheese. Serve immediately.

Serves 4

Creamy mushroom sauce and hot pasta – food that dreams are made of! And the best thing about this recipe is that it uses evaporated milk to make it creamy and so is lower in fat and cholesterol.
A green salad and crusty bread will complete your meal.

Oriental Noodles and Vegetables, Tagliatelle Salad, Creamy Mushrooms and Pasta

PEPPERONI TOSS

375 g/12 oz spaghetti
1 tablespoon olive oil
1 onion, finely chopped
90 g/3 oz black olives, chopped
125 g/4 oz pepperoni salami, chopped

It is believed that salami originated in the Grecian town of Salamis. Pepperoni, one of the most used salamis, is made from ground pork and beef and flavoured with ground red pepper. Its popularity is due to the fact that it is the salami most often used on pizza.

Pepperoni Toss

1   Cook spaghetti in boiling water in a large saucepan following packet directions. Drain, set aside and keep warm.

2   Heat oil in a large frying pan and cook onion over a medium heat for 5-6 minutes or until onion is transparent. Add olives and salami and cook for 2 minutes longer.

3   Add spaghetti to pan and toss to combine. Serve immediately.

Serves 4

Tortellini with Parsley Butter

TORTELLINI WITH PARSLEY BUTTER

500 g/1 lb tortellini
2 tablespoons olive oil
125 g/4 oz grated fresh Parmesan cheese
125 g/4 oz butter, cut into small cubes
pinch nutmeg
30 g/1 oz fresh parsley, chopped
freshly ground black pepper

1   Place tortellini and olive oil in a large saucepan of boiling water and cook following packet directions. Drain and place in a large serving bowl.

2   Top tortellini with Parmesan cheese, butter, nutmeg, parsley and black pepper to taste. Toss to combine and serve immediately.

Serves 4

There is a legend that says tortellini was created to honour Venus' bellybutton. Apparently, a Bolognan innkeeper was so inflamed with this beautiful young woman that after showing her to her room he then spied on her through the keyhole as she was undressing; but all he could see was her bellybutton. He rushed to his kitchen and created tortellini as a memento to Venus' beauty.

45

PASTA SHELLS WITH ANCHOVY SAUCE

500 g/1 lb small shell pasta
60 g/2 oz grated fresh Parmesan cheese

ANCHOVY SAUCE
2 tablespoons olive oil
3 onions, chopped
1 clove garlic, crushed
1/2 cup/125 mL/4 fl oz dry white wine
8 canned anchovies
1 tablespoon chopped fresh rosemary
leaves or 1 teaspoon dried rosemary
1 cup/250 mL/8 fl oz beef or
chicken stock
1 fresh red chilli, seeded and
cut into rings

1   Cook pasta shells in boiling water in a large saucepan following packet directions. Drain, set aside and keep warm.

2   To make sauce, heat oil in a large frying pan and cook onions and garlic over a medium heat for 10 minutes or until onions are soft. Stir in wine and anchovies and bring to the boil. Boil for 2-3 minutes or until wine reduces by half.

3   Stir in rosemary and stock and bring back to the boil. Boil until sauces reduces and thickens slightly. Add chilli and pasta to sauce, toss to combine, sprinkle with Parmesan cheese and serve immediately.

Serves 4

Anchovies come preserved in oil or salt. Once opened, canned anchovies can be kept, covered with olive oil, in the refrigerator.
Anchovies preserved in salt should be rinsed well before using.
In Italy and France fresh anchovies are popular.

MACARONI WITH TOMATO SAUCE

500 g/1 lb wholemeal macaroni

CHUNKY TOMATO SAUCE
2 tablespoons olive oil
1 onion, chopped
1 clove garlic, crushed
2 x 440 g/14 oz canned Italian-style
tomatoes, undrained and mashed
1/4 cup/60 mL/2 fl oz dry white wine
1 tablespoon chopped fresh basil
freshly ground black pepper

1   Cook macaroni in boiling water in a large saucepan following packet directions. Drain, set aside and keep warm.

2   To make sauce, heat oil in a frying pan and cook onion for 3-4 minutes or until soft. Stir in garlic, tomatoes and wine and cook, stirring constantly, over a medium heat for 5 minutes. Bring to the boil, then reduce heat and simmer, uncovered, for 10-15 minutes or until sauce reduces and thickens. Add basil and season to taste with black pepper.

3   Add sauce to hot macaroni and toss to combine. Serve immediately.

Serves 4

This fresh-tasting tomato sauce is delicious with any dried pasta. You might like to try serving it with bucatini, the Italian macaroni that is long like spaghetti, but thicker and hollow.

RED PEPPER FRITTATA

Oven temperature
180°C, 350°F, Gas 4

220 g/7 oz fettuccine
1$\frac{1}{2}$ cups/375 mL/12 fl oz milk
$\frac{1}{2}$ cup/125 mL/4 fl oz cream (double)
6 eggs, lightly beaten
2 tablespoons finely chopped
fresh parsley
1 red pepper, chopped
freshly ground black pepper

1 Cook fettuccine in boiling water in a large saucepan following packet directions. Drain and set aside.

2 Place milk, cream and eggs in a bowl and whisk to combine. Stir in parsley, red pepper, fettuccine and black pepper to taste.

3 Pour frittata mixture into a greased 23 cm/9 in flan dish and bake for 25-30 minutes or until frittata is set.

Red Pepper Frittata

Serves 4

48

Rigatoni with Pumpkin

RIGATONI WITH PUMPKIN

500 g/1 lb rigatoni
90 g/3 oz butter
250 g/8 oz pumpkin, cut into
small cubes
1 tablespoon snipped fresh chives
pinch ground nutmeg
30 g/1 oz grated fresh Parmesan cheese
freshly ground black pepper

1   Cook rigatoni in boiling water in a large saucepan following packet directions. Drain, set aside and keep warm.

2   Melt 60 g/2 oz butter in a large saucepan and cook pumpkin over a medium heat for 5-10 minutes or until tender.

3   Stir chives, nutmeg, Parmesan cheese, black pepper to taste, rigatoni and remaining butter into pumpkin mixture and toss to combine. Serve immediately.

Serves 4

You might like to make this pasta dish using carrots instead of pumpkin. The taste will be different, but just as delicious.

HAM AND CHEESE PIE

Oven temperature
180°C, 350°F, Gas 4

Another good way to use leftover pasta. This delicious pie is perfect for a winter's lunch or Sunday night tea around the fireside. Served with crusty bread and a salad of mixed lettuces and herbs, it is sure to be popular.

250 g/8 oz macaroni
3 eggs
125 g/4 oz grated tasty cheese
(mature Cheddar)
2 cups/500 mL/16 fl oz milk
1/2 cup/125 mL/4 fl oz cream
125 g/4 oz ham, chopped
1 tablespoon snipped fresh chives
freshly ground black pepper
30 g/1 oz butter

1   Cook macaroni in boiling water in a large saucepan following packet directions. Drain and place in a greased ovenproof baking dish.

2   Place eggs, cheese, milk, cream, ham, chives and black pepper to taste in a bowl and mix to combine. Pour over macaroni and dot top of pie with butter. Bake for 40 minutes or until pie is set.

Serves 4

NUTTY VERMICELLI WITH BROCCOLI

500 g/1 lb vermicelli noodles
250 g/8 oz broccoli, broken into florets
30 g/1 oz butter
4 spring onions, finely chopped
2 cloves garlic, crushed
1 teaspoon chilli paste (sambal oelek)
60 g/2 oz blanched almonds, chopped
1/4 cup/60 mL/2 fl oz white wine
freshly ground black pepper

1   Cook vermicelli in boiling water in a large saucepan following packet directions. Drain, set aside and keep warm.

2   Boil, steam or microwave broccoli until just tender. Drain and refresh under cold running water. Drain again and set aside. Melt butter in a large frying pan and cook spring onions, garlic, chilli paste (sambal oelek) and almonds, stirring, over a medium heat for 2 minutes. Stir in wine and cook for 3 minutes longer. Add broccoli and vermicelli, toss to combine and cook for 3-4 minutes. Season to taste with black pepper.

Serves 4

The crunch of almonds, the fresh taste of broccoli and a touch of chilli make a superb combination when teamed with vermicelli in this quick and easy, light meal.

Tortellini and Avocado Cream

TORTELLINI AND AVOCADO CREAM

500 g/1 lb tortellini

AVOCADO CREAM
$^1/_2$ ripe avocado, stoned and peeled
$^1/_4$ cup/60 mL/2 fl oz cream (double)
30 g/1 oz grated fresh Parmesan cheese
1 teaspoon lemon juice
freshly ground black pepper

1 Cook tortellini in boiling water in a large saucepan following packet directions. Drain, set aside and keep warm.

2 To make Avocado Cream, place avocado, cream, Parmesan cheese and lemon juice in a food processor or blender and process until smooth. Season to taste with black pepper.

3 Place tortellini in a warm serving bowl, add Avocado Cream and toss to combine. Serve immediately.

Serves 4

Avocado puréed with cream and Parmesan cheese makes a smooth rich sauce that is sure to be a hit with all avocado lovers. It is best to make this sauce just prior to serving, so that it does not discolour.

Spaghetti Carbonara

SPAGHETTI CARBONARA

There are several stories concerning the origins of this classic dish. The most romantic of these is that it was a dish created by the 'carbonari' – or charcoal makers – of Italy. The story goes that, as the dish requires little cooking and all the ingredients are transportable, the carbonari were able to cook it over an open fire.

185 g/6 oz slices ham, cut into strips
4 eggs
$^1/_3$ cup/90 mL/3 fl oz cream (single)
90 g/3 oz grated fresh Parmesan cheese
500 g/1 lb spaghetti
freshly ground black pepper

1 Cook ham in a nonstick frying pan for 2-3 minutes. Place eggs, cream and Parmesan cheese in a bowl and beat lightly to combine.

2 Cook spaghetti in boiling water in a large saucepan following packet directions. Drain spaghetti, add egg mixture and ham and toss so that the heat of the spaghetti cooks the sauce. Season to taste with black pepper and serve immediately.

Serves 4

Macaroni with Basil

MACARONI WITH BASIL

375 g/12 oz wholemeal macaroni
1 tablespoon olive oil
2 cloves garlic, crushed
250 g/8 oz button mushrooms, sliced
6 sun-dried tomatoes, drained and
cut into strips
2 tablespoons chopped fresh basil
freshly ground black pepper

1   Cook macaroni in boiling water in a large saucepan following packet directions. Drain, set aside and keep warm.

2   Heat oil in a large frying pan and cook garlic, mushrooms and tomatoes over a medium heat for 4-5 minutes. Stir in basil and season to taste with black pepper.

3   Add macaroni to mushroom mixture and toss to combine. Serve immediately.

Serves 4

Basil originally came from India, where it is still regarded as a sacred herb. It was known in ancient times in southern Europe, and in Italy it symbolised love. Traditionally, a girl would place a pot in her window as an invitation to her lover to call on her.

53

TUNA-FILLED SHELLS

16 giant pasta shells

TUNA FILLING
**250 g/8 oz ricotta cheese, drained
440 g/14 oz canned tuna in brine,
drained and flaked
$^{1}/_{2}$ red pepper, diced
1 tablespoon chopped capers
1 teaspoon snipped fresh chives
4 tablespoons grated Swiss cheese
pinch ground nutmeg
freshly ground black pepper
2 tablespoons grated fresh
Parmesan cheese**

1   Cook 8 pasta shells in a large saucepan of boiling water until al dente. Drain, rinse under cold running water and drain again. Set aside, not overlapping. Repeat with remaining shells.

2   To make filling, place ricotta cheese and tuna in a bowl and mix to combine. Mix in red pepper, capers, chives and 2 tablespoons grated Swiss cheese, nutmeg and black pepper to taste.

3   Fill each shell with ricotta mixture, and place in a lightly greased, shallow ovenproof dish. Sprinkle with Parmesan cheese and remaining Swiss cheese. Place under a preheated grill and cook until cheese melts.

These filled shells are fun to eat hot or cold as finger food, or they can be served with a sauce as a first course.

Tuna-filled Shells

Makes 16 filled shells

Spirelli with Ham

SPIRELLI WITH HAM

500 g/1 lb fresh or 410 g/13 oz
dried spirelli or spiral pasta
2 teaspoons olive oil
315 g/10 oz ham, cut into strips
6 canned artichoke hearts,
sliced lengthwise
3 eggs, beaten with 1 tablespoon grated
fresh Parmesan cheese
freshly ground black pepper

1   Cook spirelli in boiling water in a large saucepan following packet directions. Drain, set aside and keep warm.

2   Heat oil in a frying pan and cook ham and artichokes for 1-2 minutes.

3   Add spirelli to pan and toss to combine. Remove from heat and quickly stir in egg mixture. Season to taste with black pepper. Serve as soon as the eggs start to stick to spirelli – this will take only a few seconds.

Serves 4

It is said that the four-pronged fork was invented by Ferdinand II, the King of Naples, so that spaghetti could be eaten in a more refined and elegant fashion.

SALADS

*Pasta salads make wonderful starters and main
courses, and are hard to beat as an accompaniment. Served
either at room temperature or chilled, they look and taste
marvellous as picnic fare or for a buffet.*

Warm Pasta and Salami Salad

Warm Pasta and Salami Salad

250 g/8 oz large shell pasta
1 tablespoon olive oil
2 cloves garlic, crushed
60 g/2 oz pine nuts
125 g/4 oz salami, thinly sliced
1 tablespoon chopped fresh parsley

1   Cook pasta in boiling water in a large saucepan following packet directions. Drain, set aside and keep warm.

2   Heat oil in a large frying pan and cook garlic and pine nuts, stirring constantly, over a medium heat for 1-2 minutes. Remove pan from heat and stir in salami and parsley. Add salami mixture to pasta and toss to combine. Serve warm.

Serves 4 as a light meal

Warm salads are perfect for winter days when only a light meal is required. This one is great accompanied by a salad of lettuce, olives and tomatoes.

Seafood and Dill Salad

750 g/1 lb firm white fish fillets, cut into 2.5 cm/1 in cubes
2 tablespoons lemon juice
2 tablespoons finely chopped fresh dill
pinch cayenne pepper
freshly ground black pepper
125 g/4 oz spinach fettuccine
125 g/4 oz tomato fettuccine
125 g/4 oz plain fettuccine
3 zucchini (courgettes), cut into matchsticks
2 carrots, cut into matchsticks
2 stalks celery, cut into matchsticks

DILL DRESSING
1 teaspoon Dijon mustard
2 tablespoons finely chopped fresh dill
2 tablespoons lemon juice
4 tablespoons vegetable oil
freshly ground black pepper

1   Place fish, lemon juice, dill, cayenne pepper and black pepper to taste in a bowl. Toss to combine and set aside to marinate for 40 minutes.

2   Cook spinach, tomato and plain fettuccine together in boiling water in a large saucepan following packet directions. Drain, rinse under cold running water, then drain again and set aside to cool completely.

3   Steam or microwave zucchini (courgettes), carrots and celery separately for 2-3 minutes or until just tender. Refresh under cold running water and set aside to cool completely.

4   Drain fish and place fish, fettuccine, zucchini (courgettes), carrots and celery in a large salad bowl.

5   To make dressing, place mustard, dill, lemon juice, oil and black pepper to taste in a screwtop jar and shake to combine. Pour dressing over salad and toss gently. Serve immediately.

Serves 6 as a main meal

A salad of pasta and fish is a meal in itself. It makes a wonderful lunch or supper dish when served with warm crusty bread, a green salad and a glass of chilled white wine.

MULTI-COLOURED PASTA SALAD

90 g/3 oz plain shell pasta
90 g/3 oz spinach shell pasta
90 g/3 oz tomato shell pasta
6 spring onions, chopped
1 small red pepper, diced
1 small green pepper, diced

FRENCH DRESSING
2 tablespoons olive oil
4 tablespoons lemon juice
4 tablespoons white wine vinegar
$1/4$ teaspoon dry mustard powder
$1/2$ teaspoon sugar
freshly ground black pepper

1   Cook plain, spinach and tomato pasta together in boiling water in a large saucepan following packet directions. Drain, rinse under cold running water, then drain again and set aside to cool completely.

2   To make dressing, place oil, lemon juice, vinegar, mustard, sugar and black pepper to taste in a screwtop jar and shake to combine.

3   Place pasta shells, spring onions and red and green pepper in a salad bowl. Pour dressing over and toss to combine.

Serves 6 as an accompaniment

To prevent pasta that is to be used in a salad from sticking together, rinse it under cold running water immediately after draining.

CHICKEN GRAPE SALAD

250 g/8 oz small shell pasta
1.5 kg/3 lb chicken, cooked and cooled
250 g/8 oz seedless green grapes
1 tablespoon chopped fresh tarragon
3 tablespoons mayonnaise
3 tablespoons natural yogurt
freshly ground black pepper

1   Cook pasta in boiling water in a large saucepan following packet directions. Drain, rinse under cold running water, then drain again and set aside to cool completely.

2   Remove skin from chicken and discard. Strip flesh from chicken and chop. Place pasta, chicken, grapes and tarragon in a bowl and toss to combine.

3   Place mayonnaise, yogurt and black pepper to taste in a small bowl and mix to combine. Spoon over chicken mixture and toss to coat all ingredients. Serve at room temperature.

Serves 6 as a main meal

Moist chunks of chicken, green grapes and tarragon tossed in a light dressing combine the flavours of summer in this scrumptious salad.

Avocado Salmon Salad

375 g/12 oz bow pasta
1 large avocado, stoned, peeled
and roughly chopped
1 teaspoon finely grated orange rind
2 tablespoons fresh orange juice
freshly ground black pepper
4 slices smoked salmon
4 sprigs fresh dill
1 orange, segmented

1   Cook pasta in boiling water in a large saucepan following packet directions. Drain, rinse under cold running water, then drain again and set aside to cool completely.

2   Place avocado, orange rind, orange juice and black pepper to taste in a food processor or blender and process until smooth.

3   Place pasta in a bowl, top with avocado mixture and toss to combine. Roll salmon slices into cornets and fill with a dill sprig. Divide salad between four serving plates and top with salmon cornets and orange segments.

Serves 4 as a light meal

*Chicken Grape Salad,
Avocado Salmon Salad*

59

CHILLI BROAD BEAN SALAD

375 g/12 oz small shell pasta
1 tablespoon vegetable oil
250 g/8 oz shelled or frozen broad beans
1 teaspoon chilli paste (sambal selek)
1^1/$_2$ cups/375 mL/12 fl oz chicken stock
6 radishes, thinly sliced
2 tablespoons chopped fresh parsley
30 g/1 oz grated fresh Parmesan cheese

GARLIC DRESSING
^{1}/4 cup/60 mL/2 fl oz olive oil
1 tablespoon cider vinegar
1 clove garlic, crushed
freshly ground black pepper

1   Cook pasta in boiling water in a large saucepan following packet directions. Drain, rinse under cold running water, then drain again and set aside to cool completely.

2   Heat oil in a large frying pan and cook broad beans and chilli paste over a medium heat for 3 minutes. Stir in stock, bring to simmering, cover and simmer for 10 minutes. Drain off any remaining liquid and set aside to cool.

3   To make dressing, place oil, vinegar, garlic and black pepper to taste in a screwtop jar. Shake well to combine.

4   Place pasta, broad bean mixture, radishes, parsley and Parmesan cheese in a salad bowl. Pour dressing over and toss to combine.

Served with a tomato salad and garlic bread, this salad of pasta and beans with a hint of chilli makes a substantial main meal.

Serves 4 as a main meal

TUNA ANCHOVY SALAD

250 g/8 oz wholemeal pasta spirals
6 canned anchovies, drained
12 black olives
220 g/7 oz canned tuna, drained
1 tablespoon chopped fresh parsley
1 tablespoon snipped fresh chives
1 hard-boiled egg, cut in wedges

MUSTARD DRESSING
1 teaspoon Dijon mustard
1 clove garlic, crushed
1 tablespoon white wine vinegar
1/4 cup/60 mL/2 fl oz olive oil
freshly ground black pepper

1   Cook pasta in boiling water in a large saucepan following packet directions. Drain, rinse under cold running water, then drain again and set aside to cool completely.

2   Cut anchovies in half lengthwise. Wrap an anchovy strip around each olive. Place pasta, anchovy-wrapped olives, tuna, parsley and chives in a salad bowl.

3   To make dressing, place mustard, garlic, vinegar, oil and black pepper to taste in a screwtop jar and shake well. Pour dressing over salad and toss to combine. Top with egg wedges.

Serves 4 as a light meal

Made from store cupboard ingredients, this variation on a 'salade niçoise' brings together the tastes of the Mediterranean. Serve with herbed bread and a salad of mixed lettuces for an easy and stylish lunch.

CHICKEN PASTA SALAD

155 g/5 oz plain tagliatelle
155 g/5 oz spinach tagliatelle
155 g/5 oz tomato tagliatelle
2 tablespoons olive oil
2 red onions, cut into eighths
2 cloves garlic, crushed
500 g/1 lb chicken breast fillets, chopped
1 tablespoon finely chopped fresh
oregano or 1 teaspoon dried oregano
1 tablespoon finely chopped fresh basil
or 1 teaspoon dried basil
440 g/14 oz canned artichoke hearts,
drained and halved
1 red pepper, cut into strips
90 g/3 oz green olives, drained
freshly ground black pepper

Serves 6 as a main meal

Make this colourful salad of mixed pasta, vegetables and chicken in summer when fresh basil and oregano are at their best. As a final touch, top with grated fresh Parmesan cheese.

1   Cook plain, spinach and tomato tagliatelle together in boiling water in a large saucepan following packet directions. Drain, rinse under cold running water, then drain again and set aside to cool completely.

2   Heat oil in a large frying pan and cook onions and garlic, stirring, over a medium heat for 2-3 minutes. Add chicken, oregano and basil and cook, stirring, for 10 minutes longer or until chicken is cooked. Remove pan from heat and set aside to cool completely. Place cooked chicken mixture, artichokes, red pepper, olives and tagliatelle in a large salad bowl. Season to taste with black pepper and toss to combine.

VEGETABLE PASTA SALAD

500 g/1 lb small pasta shapes
of your choice
250 g/8 oz broccoli, broken into florets
250 g/8 oz cherry tomatoes, halved
6 spring onions, cut into
2.5 cm/1 in lengths
12 black olives

RED WINE DRESSING
2 tablespoons red wine vinegar
1/4 cup/125 mL/4 fl oz olive oil
2 tablespoons grated fresh
Parmesan cheese
1 clove garlic, crushed
freshly ground black pepper

Serves 8 as an accompaniment

A delicious salad that is equally good as a light vegetarian meal for four. For a garden lunch, accompany with crusty wholemeal rolls and finish with fresh fruit.

1   Cook pasta in boiling water in a large saucepan following packet directions. Drain, rinse under cold running water, then drain again and set aside to cool completely.

2   Boil, steam or microwave broccoli for 2-3 minutes or until it just changes colour. Refresh under cold running water. Drain, then dry on absorbent kitchen paper.

3   To make dressing, place vinegar, oil, Parmesan cheese, garlic and black pepper to taste in a screwtop jar and shake to combine.

4   Place pasta, broccoli, tomatoes, spring onions and olives in a salad bowl. Pour dressing over and toss to combine.

Chicken Pasta Salad,
Vegetable Pasta Salad

DESSERTS

Pasta for dessert? These two dishes make the most of pasta and provide economic and imaginative desserts – just the thing to fill hungry teenagers.

Apple Lasagne

Apricot Orange
Pudding

Apple Lasagne

64

Apple Lasagne

750 g/1¹/₂ lb green apples
30 g/1 oz butter
60 g/2 oz butter
¹/₄ teaspoon ground nutmeg
6 sheets lasagne
30 g/1 oz walnuts, finely chopped
2 tablespoons icing sugar, sifted

EGG CUSTARD
1¹/₄ cups/315 mL/10 fl oz milk
1 egg
1 egg yolk
1 tablespoon cornflour
1 tablespoon caster sugar

1 Cook lasagne in boiling water in a large saucepan following packet directions. Drain and set aside.

2 To make custard, heat milk in a saucepan and bring to simmering. Place egg, egg yolk, cornflour and sugar in a bowl and whisk to combine. Whisk hot milk into egg mixture. Return custard to saucepan and cook, stirring constantly, over a low heat for 4-5 minutes or until custard thickens. Remove saucepan from heat.

3 Spread 2 tablespoons custard over base of a shallow ovenproof dish, then layer lasagne sheets and apples into dish, finishing with a layer of apple. Pour remaining custard over lasagne and sprinkle with walnuts. Bake for 25 minutes. Serve hot or warm, sprinkled with icing sugar.

Serves 4

Oven temperature
190°C, 375°F, Gas 5

Layers of apples, lasagne and custard combine to make this filling and satisfying dessert.

Apricot Orange Pudding

125 g/4 oz dried apricots
1 cup/250 mL/8 fl oz warm water
cinnamon stick
2 tablespoons fresh orange juice
2 teaspoons finely grated orange rind
¹/₂ cup/90 g/3 oz soft brown sugar
2 teaspoons arrowroot blended with
2 teaspoons water
30 g/1 oz bread crumbs, made
from stale bread
125 g/4 oz tagliatelle
60 g/2 oz walnuts, ground
30 g/1 oz butter, melted

1 Place apricots in a bowl, pour warm water over and set aside to soak for 1 hour. Drain apricots and reserve liquid. Place apricots, 2 tablespoons reserved liquid, cinnamon stick, orange juice, orange rind and 1 tablespoon brown sugar

in a saucepan. Bring to the boil, then reduce heat, cover and simmer for 10-15 minutes or until apricots are tender.

2 Stir arrowroot mixture into apricot mixture and cook for 2-3 minutes longer or until mixture thickens. Remove pan from heat and set aside to cool.

3 Cook tagliatelle in boiling water in a large saucepan following packet directions. Drain and set aside.

4 Coat a buttered 20 cm/8 in soufflé dish with bread crumbs. Place one-third tagliatelle in base of soufflé dish and top with half apricot mixture. Repeat layers, sprinkle with walnuts and remaining sugar, and top with remaining tagliatelle. Pour butter over pudding and bake for 25 minutes. Turn onto a plate and cut into wedges to serve.

Serves 6

Oven temperature
190°C, 375°F, Gas 5

HOMEMADE PASTA

1 Place eggs in a large bowl and whisk to combine. Sift flour and salt into egg mixture.

4 large eggs
410 g/13 oz flour
large pinch salt
water

2 Using a fork first and then your hands, incorporate eggs into flour to form a coarse dough.

Here is a general rule to follow when making pasta. For a main course serving, 1 large egg to every 100 g/ $3^1/2$ oz flour, and 100 g/ $3^1/2$ oz flour per person.

3 Turn dough onto a lightly floured surface and knead by hand for 6-8 minutes or until a smooth elastic dough is formed. The dough can also be kneaded in the food processor for 2-3 minutes. Cover dough with a cloth and set aside to rest at room temperature for 15 minutes. Divide dough into manageable pieces and roll out either by hand or using a pasta machine, then use as required.

Serves 4

'Pasta is cooked when it is "al dente", that is tender but with resistance to the bite.'

FLAVOURED PASTA

TOMATO PASTA

Beat $2^1/_2$ tablespoons concentrated tomato paste into eggs, then follow method as for making Homemade Pasta.

SPINACH PASTA

Cook 75 g/2$^1/_2$ oz spinach, then drain thoroughly and squeeze to remove as much moisture as possible. Purée spinach with a pinch of nutmeg, then combine with eggs and follow method as for making Homemade Pasta.

WHOLEMEAL PASTA

Use half white flour and half wholemeal flour. Follow method as for making Homemade Pasta.

To make Herb Pasta, add 3 teaspoons of chopped fresh herbs to the eggs. Use either a single herb, such as parsley, or mixed herbs.

'Homemade pasta does not dry successfully, as the high moisture content makes the pasta dry out too quickly and crack.'

ROLLING PASTA

As well as experiencing the pleasure of making it yourself, an advantage of homemade pasta is the ranges of shapes you can create. You can roll pasta either by hand or using a pasta machine.

ROLLING BY HAND

If you are going to roll pasta by hand you will need a long rolling pin and a large work surface. Lightly flour the work surface then, using your hands, press the dough flat and roll it out, maintaining a circular shape. Keep rolling until the dough is a large thin sheet that is almost transparent – it should be thin enough to be able to read a newspaper through it! As you roll the dough, let some of it hang over the edge of the work surface – this helps to stretch it.

USING A PASTA MACHINE

1   Make the dough as for Homemade Pasta and divide dough into manageable pieces. As a general rule, divide the dough into as many pieces as the number of eggs used to make the dough. Set the rollers of the pasta machine on the widest setting and feed the dough through. Fold the rolled dough into quarters to make a square.

2   Feed the dough through the machine again, then fold again. Repeat folding and rolling of dough 4-5 times or until you have a shiny, smooth and elastic dough. Close the rollers a notch at a time and roll the dough thinner and thinner until the desired thickness is reached. Set aside to dry for 10-15 minutes.

3   To cut, using a pasta machine, feed each strip of pasta through the appropriate blades. As the strips of dough emerge from the machine catch them on your hand.

If making lasagne or filled pasta, use the pasta immediately. Otherwise, place on a clean cloth and set aside to dry at room temperature for 30 minutes or until dough is dry enough to prevent sticking, but is not brittle.

'To roll pasta by hand you need a long rolling pin and a large work surface.'

Cooking Pasta

The secret to cooking pasta is to use lots of water and a large saucepan so the pasta does not stick together.

Leftover pasta and sauces can be mixed together, then cooked in olive oil in a frying pan to make a crisp thick pancake.

Cook pasta in a large, deep saucepan of water: the general rule is 4 cups/1 litre/ 1³/4 pt water to 100 g/3¹/2 oz pasta. Bring water to a rolling boil, toss in salt to taste (in Italy, 1 tablespoon per every 100 g/ 3¹/2 oz pasta is usual), then stir in pasta. If you wish, add some oil. When water comes back to the boil, begin timing. The pasta is done when it is 'al dente', that is tender but with resistance to the bite. Remove pasta from water by straining through a colander or lifting out of saucepan with tongs or fork.

HOW MUCH TO COOK PER SERVE		
Pasta Type	First Course	Main Meal
Dried pasta	60-75 g	75-100 g
	2-2¹/2 oz	2¹/2-3¹/2 oz
Fresh pasta	75-100 g	125-155 g
	2¹/2-3¹/2 oz	4-5 oz
Filled pasta	155-185 g	185-200 g
(such as ravioli)	5-6 oz	6-6¹/2 oz

PORK AND SAGE FILLED RAVIOLI

1 quantity Homemade Pasta
dough (see recipe)
grated fresh Parmesan cheese

PORK AND SAGE FILLING
315 g/10 oz ricotta cheese, drained
60 g/2 oz lean bacon, finely chopped
155 g/5 oz lean cooked pork, finely
diced
1 teaspoon finely chopped fresh parsley
$^1/_2$ teaspoon finely chopped fresh sage
1 teaspoon grated fresh Parmesan cheese
grated nutmeg
freshly ground black pepper

To make filling, place ricotta cheese, bacon, pork, parsley, sage and Parmesan cheese in a bowl. Mix to combine and season to taste with nutmeg and black pepper. Cover and set aside while making pasta. Assemble, following directions for making ravioli.

Round ravioli can be made by cutting circles from the filled sheets of pasta.

Pork and Sage Filled Ravioli

MAKING RAVIOLI

1 On a lightly floured surface, roll pasta dough to 2 mm/^{1}/16 in thickness and cut into strips. Place strips on a teatowel or floured surface and cover with a damp cloth. Keep dough that is not being used covered.

2 Place small mounds of filling at 4 cm/ 1^1/2 in intervals along a strip of dough, then lay a second strip over the top.

3 Press dough down firmly between the mounds of filling to join the pasta. Using a zigzag pastry wheel cut the ravioli. Place prepared ravioli on a teatowel to dry for 30 minutes.

4 Cook ravioli a few at a time in boiling water in a large saucepan for 4 minutes or until 'al dente'. Drain, set aside and keep warm. Sprinkle with Parmesan cheese and serve immediately.

Half Moon Ravioli can be made by cutting the pasta dough into 5 cm/2 in circles. A small amount of filling is then placed in the middle of the circle. The circle is then folded over and the edges pressed firmly together. Dry and cook as for ravioli.

Serves 6

MAKING TORTELLINI

Cut 5 cm/2 in circles of pasta dough. Place a small amount of filling slightly to one side of the middle. Fold over circle so that it falls just short of the other side. Press edges firmly together, curve the semicircle round then pinch the edges together. Dry and cook as for ravioli.

MAKING CAPELLETTI

Remember when making filled pasta to place it, well spaced, on a teatowel to dry for 30 minutes.

Cut 5 cm/2 in squares of pasta. Place a small amount of filling in the centre of each square, then fold in half diagonally to form a triangle, leaving a slight overlap between edges. Press firmly to seal. Wrap the long side of the triangle round a finger until the two ends overlap. Press ends firmly together with the point of the triangle upright. Dry and cook as for ravioli.

CUTTING PASTA BY HAND

Before cutting, roll the pasta dough to the required thickness. For pastas such as tagliatelle, spaghetti, fettuccine and lasagne, roll dough to a 3-5 mm/^{1}/8-^{1}/4 in thickness. For stuffed pasta, such as ravioli and tortellini, roll dough to a 2 mm/^{1}/16 in thickness. Any leftover pasta trimmings can be cut into pretty shapes using a biscuit cutter; these make a wonderful garnish for soups.

TAGLIATELLE

Roll pasta dough to 3-5 mm/^{1}/8-^{1}/4 in thickness and cut into wide strips. Roll strips up loosely to form a cylinder and cut into even widths. Shake out pasta into loose nests.

Always cook pasta while making the sauce, so it can be added while it is still hot.

LASAGNE AND CANNELLONI

Roll pasta dough to 3-5 mm/^{1}/8-^{1}/4 in thickness. For lasagne sheets, cut pasta to whatever size will fit your dish. A convenient size is 10 x 12 cm/4 x 5 in. For cannelloni, cut pasta into 10 x 12 cm/4 x 5 in pieces. The cannelloni can then be cooked, filled with a stuffing and rolled before baking.

PAPPARDELLE AND FARFALLE

Roll pasta dough to a 3-5 mm/^{1}/8-^{1}/4 in thickness. To make pappardelle, using a zigzag pastry wheel cut dough into strips 2 cm/^{3}/4 in wide and 30 cm/12 in long. For farfalle, using a pastry wheel cut pasta into 5 cm/2 in squares, then pinch together the middle of each square to give a bow effect.

A large sharp knife is a must when cutting pasta by hand.

TYPES OF PASTA

Convenience of handling and storage, texture and flavour, and good cooking properties will all contribute to the type of pasta that you choose to buy and use. The following guide will help you identify and choose the best type of pasta for you.

Packaged dried pasta: Pasta asciutto comes imported or locally made. It is made from durum wheat semolina and water – labelled 'pasta di semolina di grana duro' in Italian. Eggs are sometimes used, in which case this is marked on the packet – 'all'uovo' on imported brands. Dried pasta requires rehydration as well as cooking, so requires a longer cooking time than fresh pasta.

Commercial fresh pasta: Pasta fresca, is soft and pliable and is usually sold loose. It has the combined flavours of durum wheat, semolina and eggs. Being fresh, it needs only a few minutes cooking time. Although fresh pasta keeps for only 3-5 days, it freezes well and can be kept frozen for several months. To freeze, simply divide it into serving portions, place in freezer bags, seal, label and freeze. When cooking from frozen the pasta only needs to be partially defrosted.

Prepackaged dry 'fresh' pasta: This pasta is made of eggs and should also be made from durum wheat semolina and labelled accordingly.

Pasta, in its simplest form, is a boiled dough of flour and water. In some form or other it has been a staple food of many early civilisations. In Italian, the word 'pasta' means 'dough'.

'On imported brands of pasta, "all'uovo" means that the pasta is made with eggs.'

KEY TO PASTA

1 LASAGNE: These flat sheets of pasta are most often layered with meat, fish or vegetable sauces, topped with cheese, then baked to make a delicious and satisfying dish.

2 PAPPARDELLE: This very wide ribbon pasta was traditionally served with a sauce made of hare, herbs and wine, but today it is teamed with any rich sauce.

3 FETTUCCINE: A flat ribbon pasta that is used in similar ways to spaghetti. Usually sold coiled in nests, fettuccine is particularly good with creamy sauces, which cling better than heavier sauces.

4 TAGLIATELLE: Another of the flat ribbon pastas, tagliatelle is eaten more in the north of Italy than the south and is used in the same ways as fettuccine.

5 SPAGHETTI: Deriving its name from the Italian word 'spago', meaning 'string', spaghetti is the most popular and best known of all pastas outside of Italy. It can be simply served with butter or oil and is good with almost any sauce.

6 SPAGHETTINI: This very thin spaghetti (also known as fedelini) is traditionally served with fish and shellfish sauces, but is equally as delicious served with a tomato sauce.

7 VERMICELLI: This is what the Neapolitans call spaghetti. It comes in many varieties, with very thin vermicelli being sold in clusters, and is ideal for serving with very light sauces. The longer, thicker vermicelli is served in the same way as spaghetti.

8 MACARONI: Short-cut or 'elbow' macaroni, very common outside of Italy, is most often used in baked dishes and in the ever-popular macaroni cheese.

If a suffix is added it indicates:
-ini, a smaller version;
-oni, a larger version;
-rigate, ridged; and
-lisce, smooth.

Pasta comes in an array of shapes and sizes, which can sometimes be confusing. However, many shapes are interchangeable and half the appeal of pasta is in inventing your own combinations of pasta and sauce.

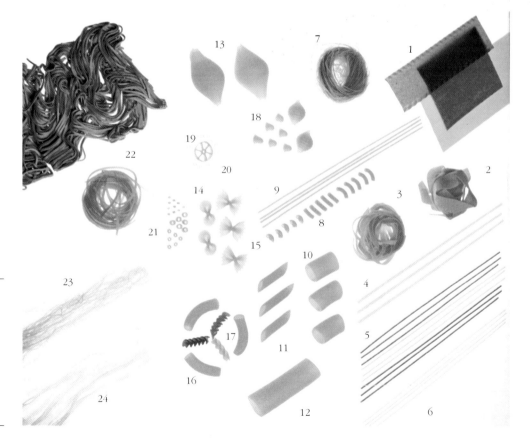

9 BUCATINI: This Italian macaroni is usually long like spaghetti, but thicker and hollow. Bucatini is used in the same way as macaroni.

10 RIGATONI: The ridges of this macaroni help sauces cling to it. It comes in many different types and is most often used in baked dishes. Rigatoni can also be stuffed and baked.

11 PENNE: A short tubular pasta, similar to macaroni but with ends cut at an angle rather than straight. It is particularly suited to being served with meat and heavier sauces, which catch in the hollows.

12 CANNELLONI: This large hollow pasta is most often stuffed, topped with a sauce and cheese then baked. Cannelloni can also be stuffed and deep-fried until crisp. If deep-frying, the cannelloni tubes will need to be boiled before stuffing and frying. Flat lasagne noodles can also be used for baked cannelloni; spread the filling down the centre of the pasta before rolling up.

13 CONCHIGLIE: A large, shell-shaped pasta ideal for stuffing. A fish filling is often favoured because of its shape. Conchiglie is often ust referred to as a shell pasta. Small shells, or conchigliette, are used in casseroles, soups and salads.

14 FIOCHETTI: This bow-shaped pasta is ideal for serving with meat and vegetable sauces, as the sauce becomes trapped in the folds.

15 FARFALLE: Meaning 'butterflies', farfelle is used in the same way as fiochetti.

16 FUSILLI: A hollow, spiral-shaped pasta that is great served with substantial meat sauces, as the sauce becomes trapped in the coils or twists.

17 TORTIGLIONI: Another spiral-shaped pasta that is used in the same way as fusilli.

18 LUMACHE: Taking its name from the Italian word for 'snail', this pasta resembles short macaroni but is larger, with a curve at one end. It is used in similar ways to conchigliette.

19 ROTELLI: This wheel-shaped pasta is added to savoury bakes, salads and soups.

20 ANELLI: Small rings of pasta usually used in soups.

21 PASTINA: There are numerous small pasta, such as anellini, ditalini and stellini. They are mostly added to soups.

22 EGG NOODLES: These flat Oriental noodles are often used in soups, while the round noodles are served with sauces and are best for stir-fries. They are also served as an accompaniment, instead of rice.

23 RICE NOODLES: Made from rice flour these noodles are served with spicy sauces and used in soups and stir-fry dishes.

24 TRANSPARENT NOODLES: Also called cellophane noodles, these noodles are added to Oriental soups and deep-fried as a garnish.

Durum wheat used in commercial pasta-making is a species of 'hard' wheat, so called because it has an endosperm rich in gluten. It has a distinctive nutty flavour and a rich amber colour. When milled to a coarsely ground meal – known as semolina – and mixed with water, the resulting dough has the characteristics ideal for commercial pasta-making.

Regional cooking traditions should not be ignored, but there are some general rules that will ensure you enjoy your pasta to the fullest: thin, long pasta needs a good clinging sauce; hollow or twisted shapes take chunky sauces; wide, flat noodles carry rich sauces; and delicate shapes require a light sauce without large pieces in it.

'The flour used for commercial pasta is made from a "hard" wheat called durum wheat.'

USEFUL INFORMATION

QUICK CONVERTER

Metric	Imperial
5 mm	$1/4$ in
1 cm	$1/2$ in
2 cm	$3/4$ in
2.5 cm	1 in
5 cm	2 in
10 cm	4 in
15 cm	6 in
20 cm	8 in
23 cm	9 in
25 cm	10 in
30 cm	12 in

MEASURING LIQUIDS

Metric	Imperial	Cup
30 mL	1 fl oz	
60 mL	2 fl oz	$1/4$ cup
90 mL	3 fl oz	
125 mL	4 fl oz	$1/2$ cup
155 mL	5 fl oz	
170 mL	$5^1/2$ fl oz	$2/3$ cup
185 mL	6 fl oz	
220 mL	7 fl oz	
250 mL	8 fl oz	1 cup
500 mL	16 fl oz	2 cups
600 mL	20 fl oz (1 pt)	
750 mL	$1^1/4$ pt	
1 litre	$1^3/4$ pt	4 cups
1.2 litres	2 pt	

METRIC CUPS & SPOONS

Metric	Cups	Imperial
60 mL	$1/4$ cup	2 fl oz
80 mL	$1/3$ cup	$2^1/2$ fl oz
125 mL	$1/2$ cup	4 fl oz
250 mL	1 cup	8 fl oz
	Spoons	
1.25 mL	$1/4$ teaspoon	
2.5 mL	$1/2$ teaspoon	
5 mL	1 teaspoon	
20 mL	1 tablespoon	

MEASURING DRY INGREDIENTS

Metric	Imperial
15 g	$1/2$ oz
30 g	1 oz
60 g	2 oz
90 g	3 oz
125 g	4 oz
155 g	5 oz
185 g	6 oz
220 g	7 oz
250 g	8 oz
280 g	9 oz
315 g	10 oz
375 g	12 oz
410 g	13 oz
440 g	14 oz
470 g	15 oz
500 g	16 oz (1 lb)
750 g	1 lb 8 oz
1 kg	2 lb
1.5 kg	3 lb

OVEN TEMPERATURES

°C	°F	Gas Mark
120	250	$1/2$
140	275	1
150	300	2
160	325	3
180	350	4
190	375	5
200	400	6
220	425	7
240	475	8
250	500	9

In this book, ingredients such as fish and meat are given in grams so you know how much to buy. It is handy to have:
🍃 A small inexpensive set of kitchen scales
Other ingredients in our recipes are given in tablespoons and cups, so you will need:
🍃 A nest of measuring cups (1 cup, $1/2$ cup, $1/3$ cup and $1/4$ cup)
🍃 A set of measuring spoons (1 tablespoon, 1 teaspoon, $1/2$ teaspoon and $1/4$ teaspoon)
🍃 A transparent graduated measuring jug (1 litre or 250 mL) for measuring liquids
🍃 Cup and spoon measures are level

INDEX

UK COOKERY EDITOR
Katie Swallow

EDITORIAL
Food Editor: Rachel Blackmore
Editorial Assistant: Ella Martin
Editorial Co-ordinator: Margaret Kelly
Recipe Development: Sheryle Eastwood, Joanne Glynn, Lucy Kelly,
Voula Maritzouridis, Anneka Mitchell, Penelope Peel,
Belinda Warn, Loukie Werle

CREDITS
Recipes page 5, 36, 37, 57, 59, 61, 65 by
Lesley Mackley © Merehurst Limited

PHOTOGRAPHY
Ashley Mackevicius, Harm Mol, Yanto Noerianto,
Jon Stewart, Warren Webb

STYLING
Wendy Berecry, Belinda Clayton, Rosemary De Santis,
Jacqui Hing, Michelle Gorry

DESIGN AND PRODUCTION
Manager: Sheridan Carter
Layout and Finished Art: Lulu Dougherty
Design: Frank Pithers

© J.B. Fairfax Press Pty Limited, 1993
This book is copyright. No part may be reproduced or transmitted
without the written permission of the publisher. Enquiries should
be made in writing to the publisher.

166 UK
Includes Index
ISBN 1 86343 044 X (pbk)
ISBN 1 85391 282 4

Published by J.B. Fairfax Press Pty Limited
Formatted by J.B. Fairfax Press Pty Limited
Output by Adtype, Sydney, Australia
Printed by Toppan Printing Co, Singapore

Distributed by J.B. Fairfax Press Ltd
9 Trinity Centre, Park Farm Estate
Wellingborough, Northants, UK
Ph: (0933) 402330
Fax: (0933) 402234

ADVENTUROUS
WINE
ARCHITECTURE

To Robert and Margrit Biever Mondavi,
for advancing the culture of winemaking and architecture

ADVENTUROUS WINE ARCHITECTURE

TEXT BY **MICHAEL WEBB**   PRINCIPAL PHOTOGRAPHY BY **ERHARD PFEIFFER**

images
Publishing

Published in Australia in 2005 by
The Images Publishing Group Pty Ltd
ABN 89 059 734 431
6 Bastow Place, Mulgrave, Victoria 3170, Australia
Tel: +61 3 9561 5544 Fax: +61 3 9561 4860
books@images.com.au
www.imagespublishing.com

National Library of Australia
Cataloguing-in-Publication entry:

Webb, Michael, 1937–.
Adventurous wine architecture.

ISBN 1 920744 33 9.

1. Wineries – Designs and plans. 2. Wineries – Pictorial works.
3. Architecture, Industrial – Pictorial works.
4. Architecture, Modern – 20th century – Pictorial works.
5. Architecture, Modern – 21st century – Pictorial works.
I. Pfeiffer, Erhard. II. Title.

725.4

Designed by The Graphic Image Studio Pty Ltd, Mulgrave, Australia
www.tgis.com.au
Scanning by Mission Productions Limited
Digital production and printing by Everbest Printing Co. Ltd in Hong Kong/China

IMAGES has included on its website a page for special notices in relation to
this and our other publications. Please visit www.imagespublishing.com.

Jacket photo of Bodegas Ysios and page 2 photo of CVNE Viña Réal ©
Erhard Pfeiffer

CONTENTS

BUILDING FOR BACCHUS

Michael Webb

The popular image of the winery remains the picturesque European château, but a growing number of winemakers around the world are seeking a fresh approach. Architects are being challenged to rethink the winery as a bold contemporary expression of tradition and innovation, agriculture and technology, production and hospitality. Many of the buildings featured here bring all these elements together in an organic whole, much as winemakers blend grapes from different lots to achieve an ideal balance in the finished product.

Over the past decade, there has been an explosion of creativity. Frank Gehry, Zaha Hadid, Renzo Piano, Steven Holl, Herzog & de Meuron, Santiago Calatrava, Rafael Moneo, Glenn Murcutt, Richard Rogers, and Norman Foster are among the acclaimed architects who have been commissioned to build new wineries or visitors' centers in California, Canada, and Australia, as well as the traditional wine-growing areas of Italy, Austria, and Spain. Some of these buildings are designed to establish brand identity and excite public attention in a fiercely competitive market; others blend into the landscape or abstract the local vernacular.

Napa Valley led the way, notably through the initiatives of Robert Mondavi, as well as by individuals and firms that are new to the business and are unconstrained by centuries of tradition. Mondavi commissioned Cliff May to design his flagship winery, and it became the area's biggest attraction—for tours, concerts, and art exhibitions. He turned to Johnson Fain for Opus One (a joint venture with Baron Philippe de Rothschild), and the Byron Winery in Santa Maria.

Others followed his example. Donald Hess, a Swiss entrepreneur, remodeled a historic stone winery as a showcase for production and his remarkable contemporary art collection. Stag's Leap Cellars commissioned new caves and tasting rooms from Barcelona architect Javier Barba. The acclaimed Swiss architects Herzog & de Meuron designed Dominus, a striking ground-up winery for the Moueix family of Château Pétrus fame. William Turnbull, an architect turned winemaker, put a fresh spin on the traditional barn, and ended his productive career with a rammed earth structure for Long

Meadow Ranch. A new generation of winemakers invited local architects to realize their vision of airy, light filled spaces, creating Roshambo and Stryker in neighboring Sonoma County.

Each of these buildings celebrates the process of turning grapes into wine, an alchemy that everyone can enjoy, and conveys a commitment to quality.

It's hard to remember that, 35 years ago when the Chappellet family designed a facility that still astonishes, there were only a handful of serious wineries in Napa Valley. California was still denigrated as a producer of cheap jug wine—in part a legacy of Prohibition and the lack of an American wine culture. Now it's a model for winemakers around the world, and graduates of the University of California Davis have taken their expertise to countries as far-flung as Israel and Japan.

More recently, the wine growing areas of Australia have performed a similar transformation, thanks to a few visionaries, massive investment, and an infusion of new blood. Quality is way up, and people drive out from Sydney, Melbourne, Adelaide and Perth to enjoy a weekend in the wine country, sampling new brands and eating as well as they would in the best city restaurants. Wine is made in almost every part of New Zealand, and this country of five million supports more than 400 wineries, which draw a steady stream of visitors, despite the lack of large population centers. In both countries, contemporary design is embraced with as much enthusiasm as innovative techniques and the latest equipment.

Across the Pacific, on a similar latitude, the wineries of central Chile and Argentina are burgeoning, and the first tentative steps are being made to reach out to visitors. In Europe, Spain is leading the way, and boasts a higher concentration of architectural excellence than any other winegrowing area. Frank Gehry's Guggenheim Museum put Bilbao on the map as the secular equivalent of Santiago de Compostella, and his visitors' center and hotel for Marqués de Riscal is likely to do the same for the quiet country town of Elciego, an hour's drive south. Already, Santiago Calatrava's dramatic showcase for Ysios and Zaha Hadid's golden pavilion for Lopez de Herredia are proving big draws. Over the past 30 years, Spain has emerged from isolation and oppression to become one of the most exciting countries in Europe, and its chefs and winemakers are companions in a voyage of discovery as exciting as that of Columbus. Curiously, the countries that led the way in winemaking are architectural laggards. France, Germany, and Portugal have the greatest legacy of classic wineries but tradition rules, stifling adventurous design.

In the Americas, and even in Europe, some wineries are intended to make an instant impression, like billboards erected to grab the attention of people driving by. Ersatz châteaux, antique palaces, and pre-Columbian ziggurat villas have nothing to do with contemporary winemaking, and everything to do with nostalgia for an idealized past. Napa Valley is full of them. Winemaker Jan Schrem invited the San Francisco Museum of Modern Art to organize a design competition for Clos Pegase. It was an inspired idea, but bright young architects submitted entries that put form far ahead of function, and Michael Graves won the commission with a huge, relentlessly symmetrical Tuscan villa that's lurid and inflexible—though undeniably a crowd-pleaser.

Architect Scott Johnson has a more reasoned philosophy of design: "Whatever you draw from the past, you have to relate to the present," he remarks. "There's a huge battle to be won when people put stainless tanks in Tuscan villas. My own approach is to use natural materials and strive for a feeling of authenticity, merging architecture and landscape. We once designed a winery for Ernest Gallo on a hillside in the Sonoma Valley. After two years of discussions, he looked at the model and asked 'when people look up the hill and see the winery, will they fall in love with it immediately?' I told him, 'I don't know. But after they've spent ten minutes driving up, stayed there an hour and driven back, they may change their minds. If they can fall in love in a minute they can just as quickly fall out of love'."

The French châteaux and German Schlösser that we so admire were all built as residences and in the language of their time. They provided a glamorous façade for the generic sheds where the wine was made. That arrangement continues to work, in Bordeaux and Burgundy, the Moselle and the Rheinland, as long as production is limited and visitors are few. But wine is now grown in every US state and almost every country in the world, and authentic châteaux are in short supply. Wines are judged more by their present quality than their pedigree, and new growers are challenging the legendary names. Novel technologies and large-scale production demand innovative facilities, and there is growing pressure to invite the public for tours, tastings, and sales. The challenge is to integrate all the elements in a whole that is greater than the sum of the parts, providing flexibility for change and growth, and straddling shifts of scale—from tank room to tasting room. The heady aroma of fermenting wine in the production areas is as exciting as the bouquet in the glass, and the best wineries offer visitors both experiences.

The essential operations of a winery are consistent and unchanging. Grapes are sorted and loaded into fermentation tanks, the fermented juice is aged in oak barrels, then bottled and shipped. The variations come in the scale of production and the winemaker's way of working. Johnson has designed four wineries and has reflected on the practical and symbolic aspects of the challenge. "Winemaking has archaic references and an immediate attachment to the earth—it's a basic process with many subtle variations," he observes. "It's a perfect program for architecture, like religion—an opportunity to create something that lifts the spirits as well as serving practical needs."

This book includes a personal selection of about thirty wineries around the world, chosen for their architectural excellence, and loosely grouped by character. All but a few were completed in the last five years. I've also included brief entries on newly completed facilities, projects under construction, unrealized proposals and one or two earlier vintages. Some roll out a welcome mat, others may be visited by appointment; a few are open only to buyers. Each offers a fresh approach to an age-old craft and an adventurous approach to building. They provide an introduction to the neophyte, a delight for the connoisseur, and they will lead you to some of the most idyllic places on earth.

EXPRESSIVE FORMS

SPAIN

CHILE

AUSTRALIA

NEW ZEALAND

ITALY

AUSTRIA

BODEGAS YSIOS

RIOJA ALAVESA, SPAIN

Santiago Calatrava, 2000–2002

Wine has been produced in Spain since time immemorial, but it has never enjoyed the international reputation of Bordeaux or Burgundy and, until recently, few landowners were willing to make substantial investments in vineyards or the latest equipment. Spain's entry into the European Community in 1985 released a long pent-up drive for expansion and experimentation. New money and talent have reinvigorated the industry. Progressive companies look to California and Australia for fresh ideas more than to France, and they have begun to use architecture as a means of communication.

Ysios is the embodiment of that spirit of adventure. Its architect, Santiago Calatrava, is a showman who combines the expressive artistry of Gaudi with the audacity of Italian engineer Pier Luigi Nervi in his bridges, train stations, museums, and exhibition pavilions. Raised near Valencia, trained in Zurich, and now practising around the world, he's an architect of dazzling facility who defies his critics and delights a broad public. His first winery is bold but disciplined, and it's an ideal fit for site and purpose.

The 80,000-square-foot winery is named for Ysis, the Egyptian goddess of wine, and is located in Rioja Alavesa, at the northern edge of Spain's premier winegrowing region. Calatrava has turned a functional production facility into an unforgettable image—a wave formation of wood and aluminum that mimics the Cantabrian mountain range to the north, and symbolizes the process of transforming grapes into wine. The curvilinear roofline minimizes the impact of this 640-foot-long building, rooting it in the rolling landscape of vineyards and pasture.

Undulating side walls provide strength with minimal bulk and the cedar boards that clad the south façade evoke wine barrels. For the roof, laminated beams of Scandinavian fir are tilted, one against the next, to produce a succession of sine curves, and are extended 30 feet out to form a prow that shades the tall, inward-sloping windows of the upstairs dining room. This prow also serves as a symbolic portico over the public entrance, which is oriented toward the medieval hill town of Laguardia, a mile to the south. Reflective aluminum cladding mirrors shifts of light and traces a wavy line that becomes the winery's signature from afar. That line is echoed in the broken mosaic rim of a reflecting pool extending the length of the building.

The 160-acre estate is planted with Tempranillo grapes which are brought up a ramp to a covered loading area at the west end of the building. There they are sorted, loaded into horizontal stabilization tanks and gravity fed to 36 cone-shaped fermentation tanks on the lower level of the building. The fermented juice is transferred to oak barrels, which are laid out in arcs at the center of the building, where the wine matures for 14–18 months before it is bottled and held for at least 36 months to earn the distinction of *Riserva*, and the premium *Vendimia Seleccionada*. The cases are shipped out from the east end, where up to 1,500,000 bottles can be stored. It's a highly efficient, slow-moving production line, which visitors can view from a mezzanine-level gallery.

Open daily. Tours by reservation. Tel: +34 945 600 640. Camino de La Hoya, Laguardia, Alava. www.byb.es

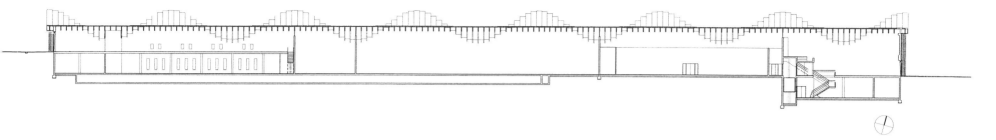

VIÑA ALMAVIVA

Spanish settlers planted vines in Chile around 1550, but over the centuries, most wine was shipped in bulk or consumed locally. With the restoration of democracy in the early 1990s, foreign capital flowed in and American and French experts helped raise the level of quality. Leading wineries introduced new technologies and turned to architects to design appropriate buildings. Exports rose from $15 million to $600 million—mostly to Europe and the United States—and wine has become a flagship industry for Chile, branded all the way to the table and projecting a favorable image of the country.

The first new wineries—replacing traditional adobe structures that succumbed to earthquakes—were generic. Viña Almaviva was one of several prestige projects that set a higher standard of excellence, along with Guillermo Hevia's Terramater, German del Sol's Viña Gracia, and Laurence Odfjell's family winery. They were commissioned by and for educated people who enjoy modern art, and their architects were encouraged to experiment and explore different styles. Wineries suddenly had cachet, and in the recession of the late 1990s talented architects were short of work. Architecture added value and told a story—something more than selling a bottle of wine.

Almaviva was named for the count in Beaumarchais' *The Marriage of Figaro*. Baron Philippe de Rothschild and Viña Concha y Toro, one of Chile's oldest firms, jointly developed this state-of-the-art facility for the production of premium wine from a 100-acre estate. Curved wood roofs unify and

harmonize two levels, and the undulating profile plays off the outline of the mountains, and the linear pattern of the vines. Within this expressive shell is a succession of bays of different length, opening off to either side of an axial concourse. By grouping these tightly together, the lines of communication are shortened and the perimeter is reduced, cutting heat loss. The design was refined over a 12-month period since the clients were slow to agree on what they wanted. However the project was realized in only 10 months, thanks to the use of prefabrication. The budget for this 42,000-square-foot winery with its 30,000-case capacity was a tenth that of Opus One (an earlier Rothschild joint-venture) and the same engineer was employed to ensure that the long spans would withstand earthquakes.

Martin Hurtado observes that "a winery has to have a distinctive spirit; it's not a factory. The production process is unlikely to change, so the building can be designed from the inside out. Beauty and harmony emerge from within, and wood allows you to work in non-standard dimensions." The architect first used laminated wood in 1993 for a car showroom while working in the forested region of southern Chile, drawing on a long tradition of using that material.

In the glass-walled reception area within the entry, carved wood figures and a hand-woven rug allude to the Mapucho Indian heritage. Beyond, to the right, is an expansive tasting room with an undulating ceiling, looking out to the vineyards. Doors open from the lobby into the axial concourse with its

quarry tile floor and elegant craft hangings, dramatically lit. The first bay contains a bottling line and bottle storage to either side. The second, concrete-framed to achieve greater height—and an odor-free interior, contains a mezzanine gallery bridging over the concourse from which grapes are gravity-fed into stainless steel fermentation tanks. The first- and second-year barrel halls occupy the third bay, and the ceiling of the first-year hall slopes down to force the perspective, as it does in the Mouton Rothschild cellars in Bordeaux. The drama of this long, tapered room is heightened by an expansive window at the far end.

Visits by appointment. Tel: +56 02 852 9300. Santa Rosa 0821, Puente Alto. www.conchaytoro.com

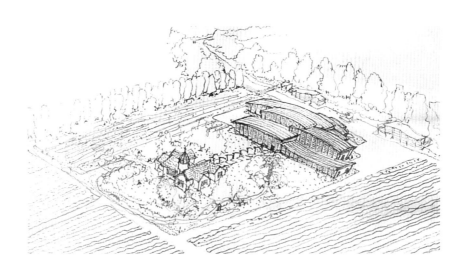

VIÑA PÉREZ CRUZ

HUELQUÉN VALLEY, CHILE

José Cruz Ovalle with Ana Turell and Juan Purcell, 2000–2002

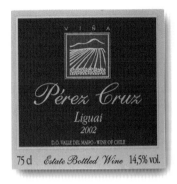

José Cruz Ovalle's sculptural wood pavilion for Chile at Expo '92 in Seville exerted great influence on his peers—and wood became a mark of national identity. Cruz, who moved to Santiago from his native Barcelona in 1987, was chosen in a limited competition, based on his feeling for the land and the Hotel Explora he designed in Patagonia, to design this innovative, 60,000-square-foot winery. It's located on a 1300-acre family farm, a quarter of which is planted with vines, a short drive from Almaviva. The architect did a meticulous series of sketches to generate the design, analyzing the relationship of land to process, and the different stages of production.

"I envisioned the building embodying the wine industry's relationship to both tradition and innovation," says Cruz. "Without being figurative, I wanted the building to be shaped by the voluptuous nature of wine and materials like wood." Inspired by the trees on the farm, he used stylized branches to support a canopy that protects the barrel-vaulted halls. The building is entirely constructed of pine and laminated wood and the projecting roof is supported on elegantly curved struts that rise from concrete posts with an infill of local stones. Three separate bays are slightly rotated and separated by covered openings that provide shade and shelter for sorting and loading.

In section, each bay comprises a pair of barrel vaulted halls linked at ground level and by a central mezzanine-level gallery. Three of the halls contain fermentation tanks, a fourth the barrel cellar, and the two to the southwest are currently used for bottle storage. The roof, tilted inward for drainage, is lofted above the barrel vaults, providing thermal insulation while allowing air and daylight to filter down from deep-set clerestories and skylights.

Approaching from across the lake in the late afternoon, Pérez Cruz resembles an enchanted forest, its sinuous branches highlighted by the setting sun. The wood has a rich glow, and the feeling of a glade dappled by shadows is carried through the interior. Few wineries capture so well the spirit of the grape or enjoy such a harmonious relationship to the land from which it comes. Cruz brings some of the exuberance of Catalonia to this remote land, while embracing its functional tradition. Wineries such as these should enjoy broad appeal, but Chile is still characterized by extremes of wealth, despite its stable government and buoyant economy, and tight security limits access. A few enlightened growers are trying to establish a wine route, here and to the south, and the number of visitors is bound to grow.

Visits by appointment. Tel: +56 2 824 2405. Fundo Liguai, Camino los Morros, Huelquen, Paine. www.perezcruz.com

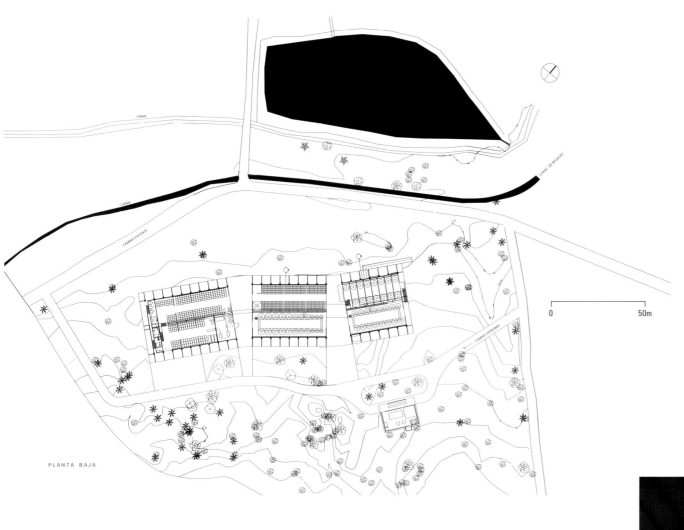

PLANTA BAJA

Volviendo sobre las observaciones del campo y de la vegetación nativa dibujada en el lugar: los apretados ramajes que desde el suelo se abren hacia lo alto dejando atrapado el espacio, el aire entre ellos — tal espesor.

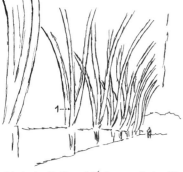

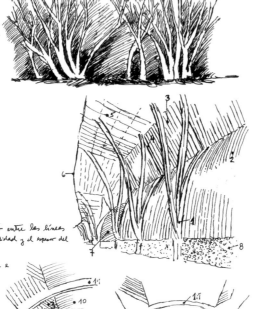

1. La triple estructura abriéndose con el aire atrapado entre las líneas voluptuosas de sus curvas para constituir la profundidad y el espesor del borde, perímetro

2. Las tablas curvadas del cerramiento de las bóvedas

3. los ritmos de aire y luz en las celosías de ventilación e iluminación

4. Piezas entre celosías

5. Ritmos de la estructura de la cubierta

6. Lo levemente sinuoso del borde del alero

7. Superficies formadas con machihembrados

8. Zócalo de piedras del lugar — rugosidad

9. Aletas pantallas del lucernario

10. Superficies machihembradas de la bóveda

11. Arco de la estructura

Todas estas como variaciones del tamaño, la retención de luz... grados y graduaciones de la textilidad y visualidad en los matices de la luz y sombra ---> la forma de la voluptuosidad

JCL
2000/2001

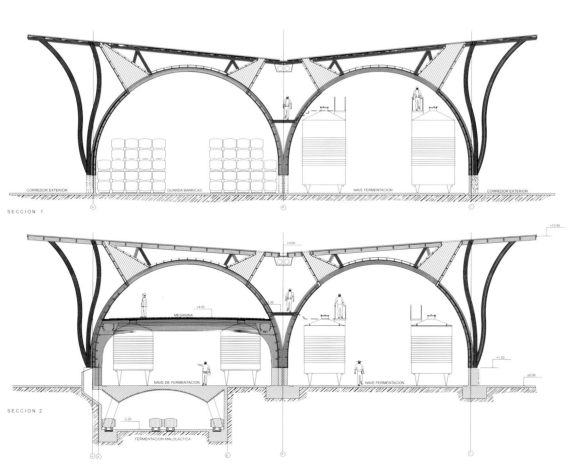

CORREDOR EXTERIOR   GUARDA BARRICAS   NAVE FERMENTACION   CORREDOR EXTERIOR

SECCION 1

MESANINA

NAVE DE FERMENTACION   NAVE FERMENTACION

FERMENTACION MALOLACTICA

SECCION 2

TEMPUS TWO

Rivalry between the two principal Australian cities is reflected in the competition between their wine growing areas: Hunter Valley, a two-and-a-half-hour drive north of Sydney, and Yarra Valley, which begins just north of Melbourne. Hunter lagged, in quality and popular appeal, but is now striving to catch up. Tempus Two, located at a major interchange on a gently sloping site, is a measure of how far the area has come. Designed as a showcase for the premium brand of McGuigan Wines, it quickly became a destination—in part because the wine is sold only at the cellar door and in three select restaurants. The architecturally exuberant winery offers tours and a spacious tasting room, the Asian-fusion Oishii restaurant, and a natural grass amphitheater seating 7000. This was inaugurated by Dame Kiri Te Kanawa, an event that drew music lovers from all over the region.

Design director Philip Manss worked with project architect John Bakker, and they make the creative process sound easy. "After the first meeting, I'd opened a bottle of Pinot Gris and was watching footy on TV when I took out a notepad and began doodling," Manss recalls. The design hardly changed from that first sketch." The goal was to break up the bulk of the 25,000-square-foot facility by dividing different functions among seven linked pavilions arranged in an arc within a natural gully. Each is a stylized version of the traditional country shed, a utilitarian typology that has inspired many Australian architects, with pitched roofs and walls of insulated coolant panels faced with zinc.

Jutting steel canopies (cable-braced to pylons above and posts below) and canted façades of black concrete slabs face onto an elliptical plaza. A tilted polycarbonate canopy covered with vines extends around the outer edge of the plaza, shading outdoor tables, and a free-standing canopy, flanked by fountains on axis with the entry drive, provides a symbolic portico for the central tasting room. Pavilions to the left are used for storage, fermentation and as a barrel room; the restaurant and reception areas are to the right. Behind the uniform façades, the pavilions are of different heights and lengths, and can be extended back into the service/loading area to the rear. Rainwater is collected off the roofs into tanks, and is drained from hard surfaces into an artificial lake that is used to irrigate the 75-acre estate.

Suters has created a meticulously detailed monument from simple shapes and unpretentious materials. Pewter-painted doors to each pavilion hint at the pewter foil wine labels that are imported from Italy. The tasting room/sales area has a polished floor of concrete mixed with silica fume to create a hard, impervious surface with a marble-like finish. The exposed metal walls and ceiling service ducts are foils for the textured slate tiles on the face of the stainless-topped bar, with its dramatically backlit niches containing wine bottles. Parke Withers designed the lounge with its soft leather sofas and patterned walls and a coffee bar is located next door.

Open daily. Tours by appointment. Tel: +61 2 4993 3999. Corner of Broke Rd. & McDonalds Rd, Pokolbin, New South Wales. www.tempustwowinery.com.au

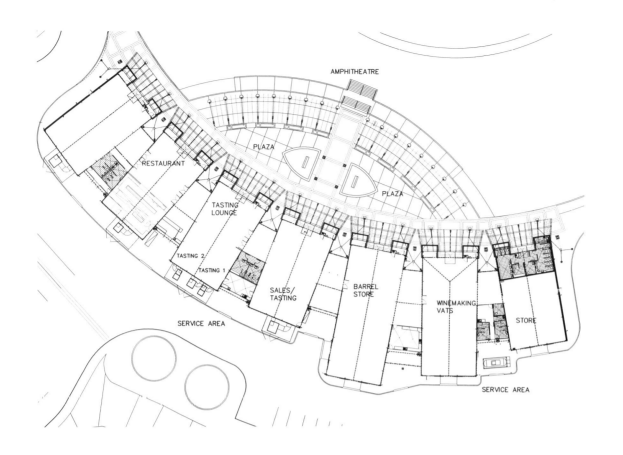

AMPHITHEATRE

PLAZA

PLAZA

RESTAURANT

TASTING LOUNGE

TASTING 2

TASTING 1

SALES/ TASTING

BARREL STORE

WINEMAKING VATS

STORE

SERVICE AREA

SERVICE AREA

OISHII

SILENI ESTATES

Dodd Paterson + Bukowski Rehm
1997–1999

Another sophisticated tin shed, but on a vastly greater scale, Sileni sweeps everything under one big pitched roof. Graeme Avery, former CEO of a medical publishing company, and his wife Gaby, chartered accountant Chris Cowper, and winemaker Grant Edmonds established this winery as a destination that would combine quality with quantity, and boost wine tourism in Hawkes Bay. The region has much to offer, but it's four hours on narrow roads from Auckland and Wellington, the two major cities on the north island. Sileni (which is named for Roman vintage deities associated with Bacchus) is worth the drive—for its wines, exemplary cuisine, gourmet store and cookery lessons.

Sileni has the capacity to produce 80,000 cases of premium Semillon and Merlot from the adjoining vineyard, as well as Pinot Noir and Chardonnay from a higher, cooler location. That's big-time for a country that focuses on quality varietals for the export market, and charges a higher average price for its wines even than France. Edmonds is a dedicated professional with a breezy manner who looks forward to the vintage because "I can tell everybody to bugger off, put my overalls on and get out there."

Dodd Patterson had designed three houses for Avery over 30 years, so they understood what their client wanted. The architects created an industrial shed of corrugated zinc that catches the light and turns white, reducing its impact on the land but standing out against the hills to the rear. It is set far back from the road at the end of a long, straight drive, and the silvery façade blends into the hill behind, so that the theatricality of the 27-foot-high portico (extended forward from the vault of the tank room) becomes apparent only as you approach and park around the circle with its grass triangle—a motif inspired by the shape of the triangular vineyard and repeated in the portico.

Walking around, you discover how far the building extends back on its river-rock base, accommodating 23-foot-high tanks at the center, barrels and storage to the sides. You glimpse the tanks through a window at the rear of the lofty atrium and from the staircase that ascends to the first-floor library and offices, and the second-floor boardroom, which commands a panoramic view of the valley through windows that open on three sides. The basement gourmet store opens into a tasting room with vintage French winemaking memorabilia. The Mesa restaurant occupies the front of one wing, and its tables spill out into an orchard. A banqueting space occupies the other wing.

Open daily. Tel: +64 6 879 8768. 2016 Maraekakaho Road, Hastings. www.sileni.co.nz

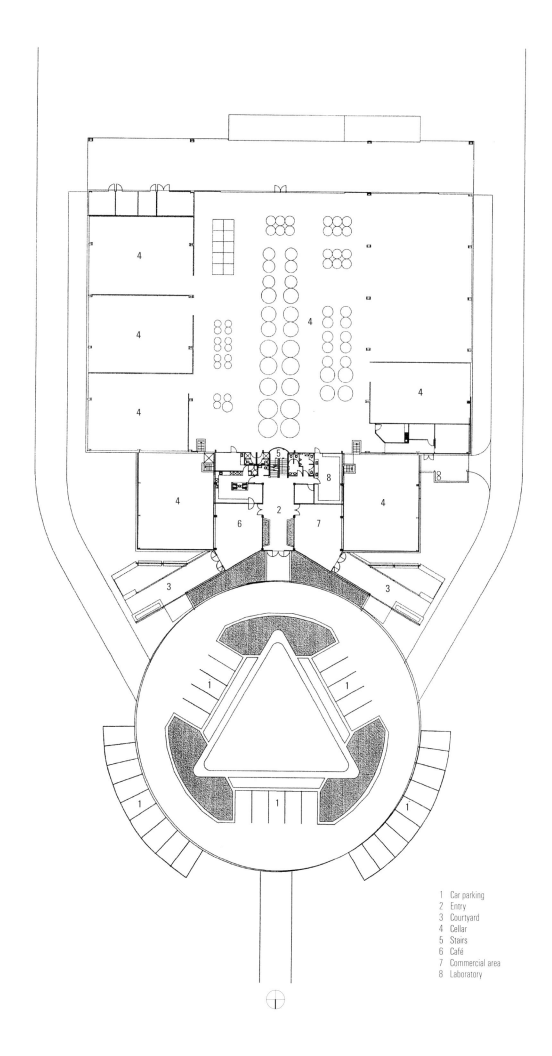

1 Car parking
2 Entry
3 Courtyard
4 Cellar
5 Stairs
6 Café
7 Commercial area
8 Laboratory

CRAGGY RANGE GIANTS WINERY

HAWKES BAY, NEW ZEALAND

Blair & Co, 1999–2002

A spectacular showcase that is named for the jagged hills of Te Mata —a dead giant in Maori legend—across the road to the west, and to distinguish it from the Gimblett Block winery, where most of Craggy Range wines are made, Giants specializes in Bordeaux varietals under direction of winemaker Steve Smith. It's a visionary project conceived by Terry Peabody, an American businessman based in Brisbane, who considered locating in California, France, and Australia before choosing Hawkes Bay. He interviewed ten high-profile architects and chose John Blair, who was best-known for ski buildings and high-end houses, but is now designing several more wineries. Blair, Peabody, and Smith went off to Napa and France searching for fresh ways of combining innovation with tradition.

Blair enjoyed great freedom and a $14 million budget, working closely with Smith. He stood on a peak looking down over the valley and realized he had to break up the mass and use gable roofs to relate the buildings to their neighbors. Mountains and the Tukituki River on the opposite side of the estate dictated a north–south axis, with buildings sliding past each other, relating to the long lines of vines. "It's serious business, not a trophy building, and I was able to plan, design, and furnish it," says the architect. "It's important you make people feel good and give them a chance to learn something."

Sharp-edged buildings of stone, stucco and colorbond (corrugated, powder-coated steel) are grouped in a picturesque, linear formation, and reflected in an artificial lake. A conical vaulted rotunda houses Terroir, a Provençal-style restaurant, linked by a lattice frame to an expansive cellar door with upstairs offices. A stone portico with an upstairs boardroom is set forward from a domed rotunda. The tank room juts out to the right. These disparate buildings are reflected in a pond set in an acre of grass and trees. The "Giants" label seems apt, for each element of the composition has its own imposing character. There's a strong postmodern flavor, though the complex is quirky and engaging, and a reticent building would be entirely overwhelmed by the sculptural drama of Te Mata.

The architect speaks of combining high tech and romantic imagery to symbolize hospitality and production. He chose materials for their texture and warmth. Hinuera (sedimentary volcanic) stone from Hamilton was employed for paving in its pale natural state, and it was fired golden brown to bring out its strong markings for the walls. This tone complements the burnt hills of late summer. Slate-colored terracotta shingles or low-gloss steel sheet are designed to minimize reflections. A dark zinc-clad dome is housed within a pine-framed canopy, evoking grain silos and hay barns. The interior, lit from the roof lantern, contains a circle of 8000-liter French oak vats raised above the stone floor. A spiral stair leads up to catwalk and a laboratory—a light-filled command post. A curved stone stair leads down to the barrel cellar with its poured concrete walls and arched vaults, inspired by those at Château Meursault.

Blair is currently building Te Awangwe, a low range of buildings clad in patinaed copper, for a German couple in Hawkes Bay, and is designing other prestigious wineries.

Open daily. Tel: +64 6 873 7126. 253 Waimarana Road, Havelock North. www.craggyrange.com

RETAIL SALES

ENTRY

RECEPTION

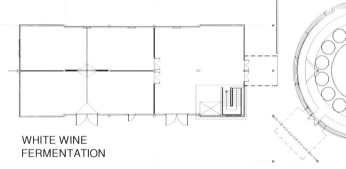

WHITE WINE
FERMENTATION

RED W
FERM
(CELL

VITICU

RESTAURANT

EPICUREAN
SCHOOL

STAFF
AMENITIES

CITTADELLA DEL VINO

TRENTINO, ITALY

Alberto Cecchetto, 1998–2000

Building in northern Italy is like making changes in a venerable museum, which is why so many Italian architects limit themselves to the design of furniture or finely detailed interiors. Too often, new construction has to conform to the appearance of what is already there, which stifles the inventive spirit that flourished in Italy for two millennia. Cittadella del Vino is a notable exception to this timidity: a bold, contemporary expression of large-scale production. Even more surprising, architect Alberto Cecchetto is based in Venice, where little of note has been built in the past hundred years.

Located to the north of Trento, the new complex was commissioned by the MezzaCorona group to celebrate the centenary of its founding, consolidate its operations, and achieve a higher level of quality. The group began as a cooperative of 30 growers producing bulk wine, and has expanded to 1600 growers and an annual production of up to 1.8 million cases of still wine, and a smaller quantity of Cantina Rotari *metodo classico* sparkling wine. The forecourt is flanked by a low, grass-roofed shop and tasting area, a sunken auditorium and a three-story block of offices that are shaded by a canted screen of steel mesh. A tilted cone of steel tubes wraps around an elevator.

That's the public face, but the model factory to the rear is equally impressive. Undulating laminated wood beams are supported by cables from posts in an echo of the stakes that support the acres of vines on the neighboring hills. These provide long, unbroken spans in the skylit production areas, pulling in light and air to the separate loading, fermentation and bottling areas for the still and sparkling wines. The glass-walled offices are bathed in softly filtered light and enjoy sweeping views out to the rolling hills and distant mountains. Dinners are catered in intimate, bottle-lined rooms that lead out of the production areas—much like a chef's table that places guests at the heart of the action. The auditorium and outdoor amphitheater also serve to generate revenue and provide an amenity for the region.

Open daily. Tours by appointment. Tel: +39 0461 613 300. Via del Teroldego 1, Mezzocorona. www.mezzacorona.it

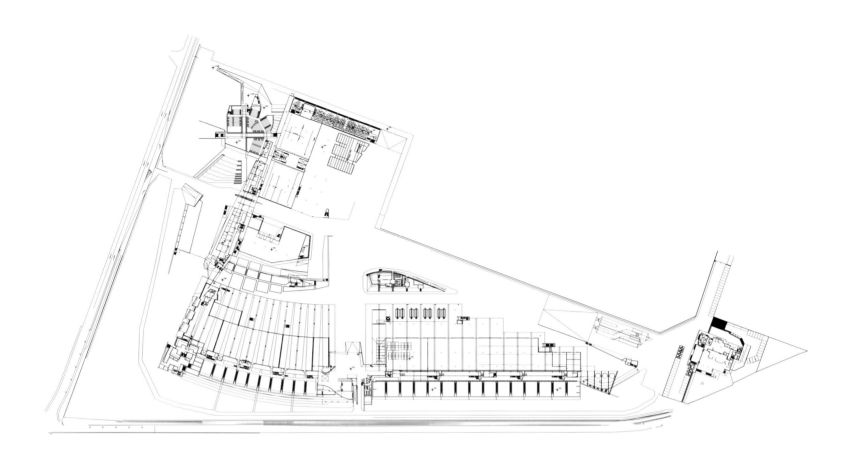

LOISIUM

GRÜNER VELTLINER
KARL STEININGER, AUSTRIA
STEVEN HOLL, NEW YORK

The Steininger family-run winery, and two other families from the small town of Langenlois came together to create Loisium, a portal to the wine culture of the region, an hour's drive west of Vienna. The goal was to find a new use for the wine cellars, some dating back to AD 1100, that form a labyrinth beneath the postcard-pretty town, together with a center for visitors and community events, and an exclusive hotel-restaurant.

To everyone's surprise, this provincial enterprise hired New York architect Steven Holl, and gained an architectural masterwork. He translated the geometry of the tunnels, cut from the soft loess rock, into wall fissures that light an aluminum-clad, 12,000-square-foot cube of reinforced concrete. The slits frame fragments of the landscape. Steps thread though three levels of the interior, linking a rooftop terrace, offices, a sales area, tasting bar and cafeteria. Glazed openings in the bottom of a reflecting pool light the subterranean passage leading back from a tour of the dramatically enhanced vaults.

"When I presented my first sketch I thought: 'there's no way they're going to want this'," says Holl. "There were only five people in the room, and the mayor said: 'we're going to build this and the hotel.' He is the building department; they drew the [zoning] envelope based on my drawing. It helped that I wasn't from Vienna, and that I was the first foreign architect to work in the area. The wife of one of the sponsors was Finnish, and she knew me from Kiasma, the contemporary art museum I did in Helsinki."

Holl has a gift for adding subtle moves to simple forms, investing a prosaic program with poetry. The angular stainless steel plates of the skin shed rain and snow, amplify the geometry of the openings, and respond to shifts in light through the day and in different seasons. At his wife's suggestion, he tilted the cube five degrees toward the vaults, so that it beckons you forward to the path that leads through the rows of vines. Slumped green glass inserted into the slit windows mediates between the green of the vines and of the bottles on the racks of the sales area. The pool dapples the light entering the tunnel that leads back from the vaults.

Even if you've seen photographs and know some of Holl's other work, the Loisium comes as a shock. The silvery cube is scale-less, and it takes its cues from the ancient network of passages, not the streets and ornamental façades that cluster around the baroque church. The asymmetrical gashes in its sides suggest the fractures of an earthquake, at least to a visitor from California. At once it's futuristic and archaic, and to the elderly Austrians piling out of their tourist coaches it must look as strange as a spaceship. There's a great deal of muttering and shaking of heads. Once inside, they are reassured. The cork walls are soft to the touch; there are things to buy, and a place to sit and eat while gazing out over the orderly rows of vines. The gashes seem less harsh, and they concentrate the views. There are exciting vistas from one level to another, and the displays seem to hover in the soft light. When tourists emerge to take the underground tour, they've

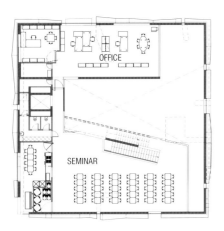

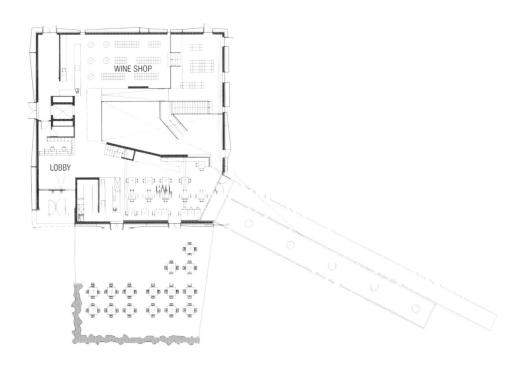

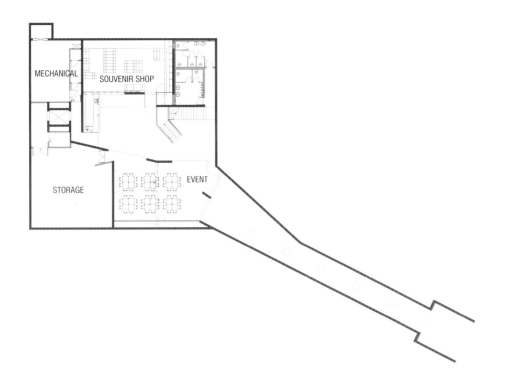

revised their first opinions, and see how the metal changes color in the sun and shimmers in the pool. From afar it becomes a gleaming sculptural object, a work of art that enriches the landscape.

Loisium has had a Bilbao effect on the public perception of Austrian wines. The industry was hard hit by the adulteration scandal in 1985, which wiped out most low-cost producers. Production was on too small a scale to make an impact beyond the country, but new growers have made a virtue of smallness. Gruner Veltliner, the dominant Austrian white wine varietal, has begun to build a cult following abroad. A recent exhibition at the Architecture Center in Vienna featured forty adventurous new Austrian wineries, designed by native architects.

Open daily, except in January. Tel: +43 02734 32240.
Loisiumallee 1, Langenlois. www.loisium.at

MARQUÉS DE RISCAL

RIOJA ALAVESA, SPAIN

Gehry Partners, 1999–2006

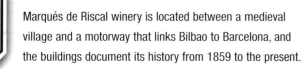

Marqués de Riscal winery is located between a medieval village and a motorway that links Bilbao to Barcelona, and the buildings document its history from 1859 to the present. The newest addition (by Frank Gehry and project architect Edwin Chan), which combines a visitors' center, restaurant, and exclusive hotel, should tilt the balance toward the future when it's completed, early in 2006. The winding lanes are likely to fill with cars and tour buses, as visitors drive the 90 miles from the Guggenheim to inspect the master's latest wonder. They may round off their tour with a visit to Ysios, but even Calatrava cannot match the extravagance of Gehry's invention.

The winery claims to be the oldest and most innovative in the region, and it is also one of the largest, with plans to increase its annual production of 375,000 cases of *Riserva* and *Gran Riserva* red and rosado, in addition to the premium brand of Baron de Chirel, made in selected years from old vines. The estate comprises 540 acres, but Riscal controls 3300 more, giving it the resources to plan an ambitious program of modernization. The goal is to integrate old and new, combining quality with quantity.

Beyond a forbidding façade of grim warehouses and barred gates is a new tank room that has been built into the hillside to reduce its impact. An undulating wood canopy provides shade as the grapes are unloaded and hints at what is to come. Computers in a central control booth set temperatures in the 151 stainless tanks on the upper level, and the 76 below, which are used for a second fermentation. Old buildings have been remodeled and brightened to serve as offices. "The winery is a series of buildings," said production director Francisco Hurtado, a descendant of the winery's founder. "To join them so that visitors can come on a coherent circuit, we've asked for Gehry's help." The first concept was a quiet link in stone, plaster and wood, but the project took on a life of its own as the program changed.

The tank room is hunkered down but the new structure floats free on elevated ground, conducting a dialogue with the medieval stone church across the valley, and expanding its presence far beyond the 25,000 square feet it encloses. Curved titanium wrappers in gold and tones of red pick up on the colors of the grapes and vines, and embrace boxy sandstone volumes. The building is raised on three clustered columns to shade an entry plaza, which leads to a reception area, bar, and a terrace from which visitors can enjoy sweeping views of the vineyards and spectacular landscapes. Guest bedrooms, a restaurant with outdoor dining terraces, and conference rooms occupy the three upper levels.

Visits by appointment. Tel: +34 945 60 60 00. Calle Torrea 1, Elciego.
www.marquesderiscal.com

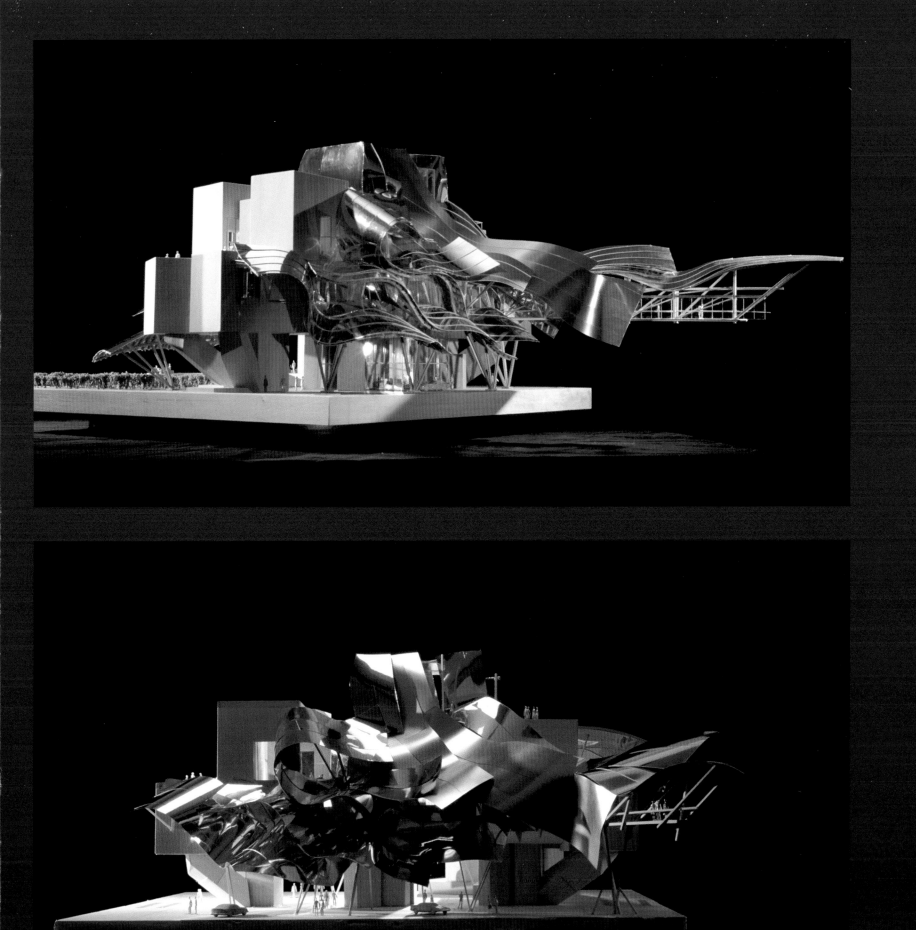

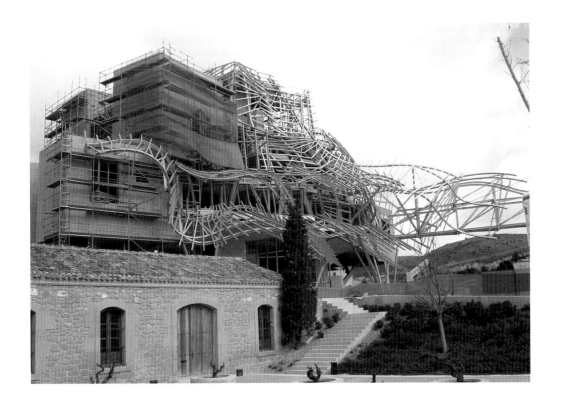

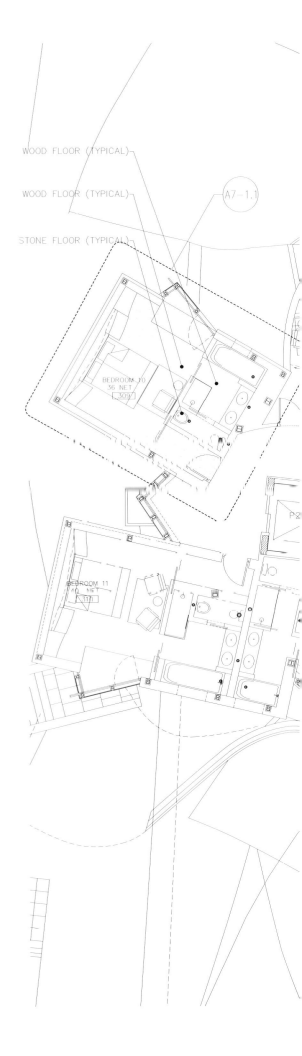

WOOD FLOOR (TYPICAL)

WOOD FLOOR (TYPICAL)

A7-1.1

STONE FLOOR (TYPICAL)

BEDROOM 10
36 NET
309

P2

BEDROOM 11
40 NET
311

OUT OF THE EARTH

USA

ITALY

CHILE

ARGENTINA

SWITZERLAND

AUSTRALIA

DOMINUS

N APA V ALLEY , C ALIFORNIA

Herzog & de Meuron, 1995–1998

Christian Moueix, a scion of the family that made Château Pétrus one of the world's most coveted wines, acquired an interest in the 124-acre Napanook Vineyard, and released his first vintage of Dominus in 1983. Several architects were considered for the design of a new winery before Jacques Herzog and Pierre de Meuron (who would win the 2001 Pritzker Architecture Prize), were selected. Christian Moueix's wife, Cherise, an American who ran an art gallery in Paris, explained her choice of the Swiss architects: "They had worked on inexpensive projects and we had a limited budget, they have a European point of view and take their cues from the site rather than doing signature buildings, and they were our generation so we could be at ease with them. Best of all, they are great wine fans, and wanted to give us the best instrument possible for making good wines."

The winery was to be a production facility that would anticipate future needs within a single building, and provide a linear progression from the delivery of grapes to the shipping of bottles. Four rows of barrels—one atop the other at the center, a single row at the edges, in the French manner— determined the 82-foot width of the building; the output of the different parcels of the estate determined the number of tanks (57 in different sizes) and the amount of storage, and those three components set the 333-foot length. As for the language of the building, Edouard Moueix explained: "My father wanted an invisible building that would be an expression of the land. Our aim is to produce great fruit—the winery is just a facility for turning this into great wine."

Herzog and de Meuron proposed three concrete containers clad in recycled railroad ties, but it proved impossible to eliminate the odor of tar in the wood. Inspired by the pierced screens of Islamic buildings, which protect from sun yet allow air to flow freely through, they came up with gabions—wire cages containing rocks that are used to check avalanches beside mountain roads in Switzerland. To demonstrate their beauty, they assembled a stack in their office in Basel, and commissioned a local builder to erect a trial wall on site. The design review board was initially skeptical but was won over, and construction went forward, using imported Swiss cages filled with locally quarried dark basalt. "The gabions create an above-ground cave, where the wine is surrounded by a stone mass that breathes," says Herzog.

Paradoxically, the building excites curiosity because of its minimalism. From Route 29, the main artery of Napa Valley, it resembles a dry-stone wall with two wide openings, slicing across the vineyard and merging into the Mayacamas Mountains beyond. Invited guests who pass through the gate and up the axial drive, discover that the façade comprises smaller rocks at the base, and a mesh grill and open slot lighting the offices at the upper right. The openings between the three blocks serve as frames, leading the eye forward to the vineyards, and then, close-up, become permeable. What appears solid from afar dissolves as you approach and enter. Massive yet airy, it is a building in which structure and skin are integral and rooted in the earth.

The opening to the left serves as a protected crush pad, and mechanical equipment is concealed within the south end of the building to leave the roof uncluttered. A dense mesh at the base excludes snakes, and distress calls are played to keep birds away. Plexiglas panels admit dappled light

but shut out vermin, and can be removed to evacuate vapors from the tank room. Smaller rocks provide greater thermal insulation and the barrel room is lined with concrete to maintain a consistent temperature. A tasting room of monastic restraint with an oak refectory table, suspended period light bulbs, and a single bronze sculpture overlooks the barrels.

On the second floor, above the storage areas, are offices for six, the lab, and a meeting/lunch room opening onto an enclosed terrace. Cherise Moueix admired the glass boxes of artist Dan Graham, and the architects used those as a model for the office area. Floor-to-ceiling glass is set into the polished concrete floor and fine mesh ceiling with Swiss precision, providing a juxtaposition of rough and refined, and capturing great views and reflections of the varied terrain. An outer corridor wrapped around these rooms within the brise soleil on the façade shades them from the harsh sun and allows cool air to circulate, which adds to the energy efficiency of the building.

A restrictive use permit prevents Dominus from welcoming visitors. Yountville, California. www.dominusestate.com

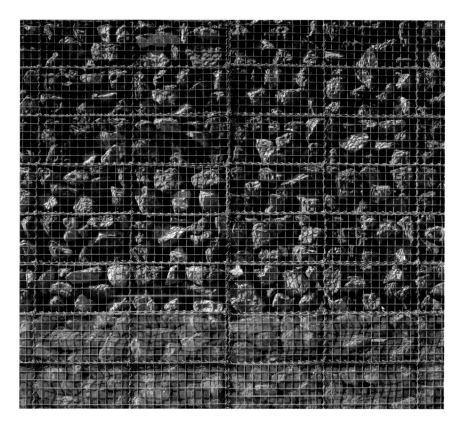

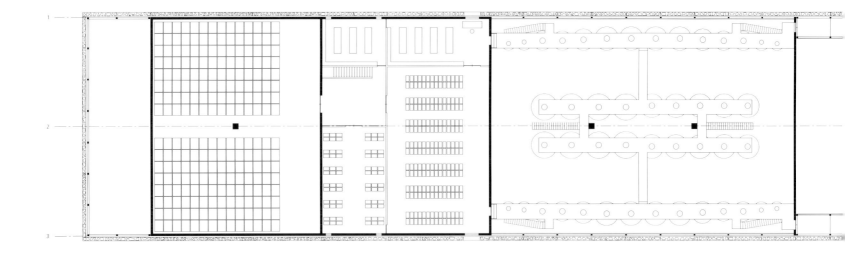

CA'MARCANDA

TUSCANY, ITALY

Giovanni Bo, 1998–2001

This is the authentic, rural Tuscany, far removed from the roar of tourist buses: a gently rolling landscape, sandwiched between the Tyrrhenian Sea and the Apennines, studded with olive and cypress, and seemingly little changed since Renaissance painters used it as a backdrop for their Madonnas and princely portraits. Appearances are deceptive. The Maremma was a malarial marsh until it was drained in the 1950s, and it has only recently become one of Italy's most prestigious wine regions. Angelo Gaja, a fourth-generation winemaker from Barbaresco, planted 150 acres of Cabernet and Merlot, and commissioned architect Giovanni Bo, who had worked with him for many years, to design a winery for the production of 20,000 cases of premium wine. The goal was to match the excellence of the wines his family has made for more than a century in their native Piedmont, and more recently in Montalcino, Tuscany.

"Working the vineyards is much easier here than at home," says Gaja. "The Langhe with their steep hillsides seem to me like a tough school lesson. On Tuscany's coast it's like a vacation; everything goes easily!" He gave one of his new blends the name Magari (a phrase Italians use with a shrug when they are betting on something), along with Promis, and the exclusive Ca'Marcanda. Bo, who is in his seventies and practises in Asti, created a 95,000-square-foot winery that is as efficient as it is beguiling; a work of art that is one with the land.

From the gate, one glimpses a low building faced with rough stones from the site, the outward expression of a winery whose two main production levels are buried in the hillside beyond. Centuries-old olives, cleared when the vines were planted, surround the property. A lawn extends over the covered loading area; angled copper roofs push up above angular steel porticoes. At a distance it could be another cluster of farm buildings. Close-up you can appreciate the meticulous detailing of simple materials. A black lacquered steel column supports the entry façade, and these same pipes (recycled from a Czech aqueduct) are employed throughout. Bronze-framed picture windows reflect Bo's abstract iron sculpture in the forecourt and light an expansive lobby, which is separated from the conference/tasting room by a folded screen wall of lacquered steel, similar in finish to the glossy black basalt floor tiles.

The same materials are carried through the upstairs offices and lower-level production areas, which are spacious and spotlessly clean. Bo used a 27 x 27 foot module for the working areas, and contributed freestanding artworks—from a sculptural steel hearth to a cloud of silver metallic mesh wrapped around light wands in the stairwell—to enrich the complex. And yet, every feature and surface is functional. Down lights are bracketed to the steel columns. Elaborate canopies of rusted iron strips provide shady porticoes and evoke old barns. In time they should turn a reddish-green hue and merge with the local vegetation. Small plastic containers of grapes are brought in by forklift and tipped through floor openings into tanks on the level below. (Must is transported to Piedmont and turned into grappa). The tiles can be easily washed down, and the floor of the barrel room is cooled to avoid cluttering the concrete-tile ceiling. A glass screen separates the bottling line from the fermentation tanks.

Not open to the public. Tel: +39 0565 76 38 09. Loc. S. Teresa, Castagneto Carducci. gajad@tin.it

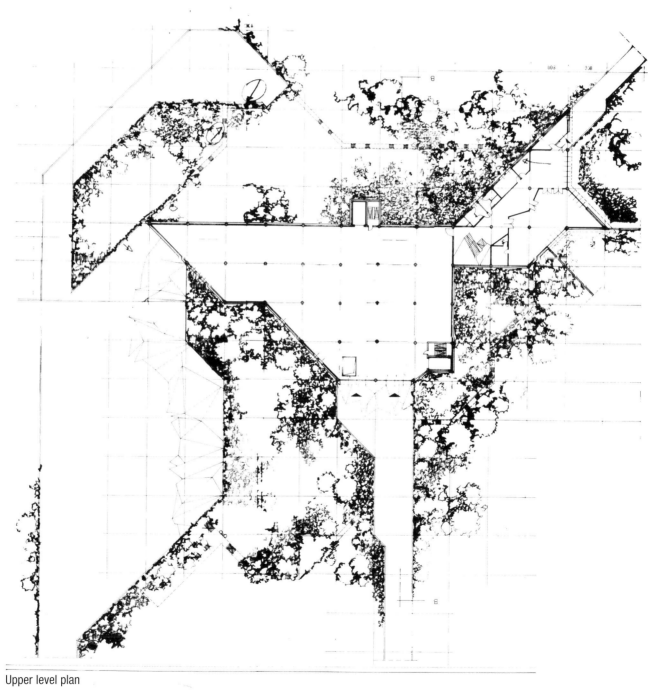

Upper level plan

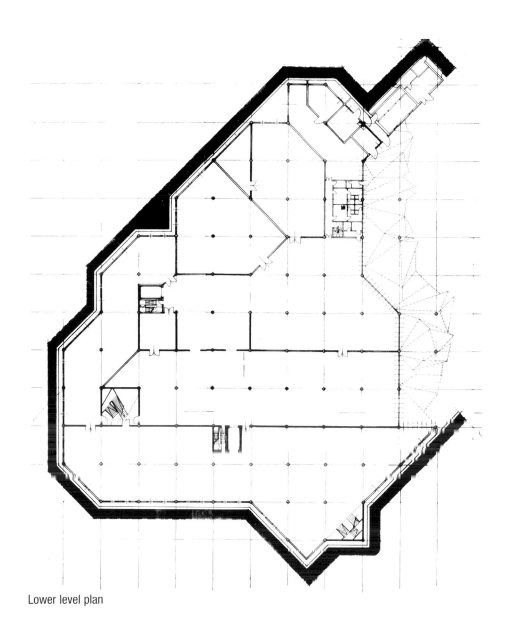

Lower level plan

VIÑA MATETIC

SAN ANTONIO VALLEY, CHILE

**Laurence Odfjell & Rodrigo Ferrer
2002–2004**

The incredible disappearing winery: so tightly integrated into a hilly landscape that, from the approach road, you see nothing but a low horizontal roof. Matetic is located 40 miles west of Santiago in a new winegrowing area near the ocean. It was commissioned by a family of Croatian origin, who own much of the surrounding land and wanted to express the spirit of organic farming. Visitors park above the winery and walk down a curved ramp to a broad terrace overlooking the valley. Beyond the glass fronted entry lobby are three glass enclosures looking down into sunken tank rooms. Small tanks with a maximum capacity of 5000 liters are gravity-fed from the terrace, and the winery has a capacity of 40,000 cases a year. Gently-curved laminated beams support a canopy that protects the terrace and reaches back to the rear wall to shade the walkway. A standing-seam copper roof picks up on the linear pattern of the vines. Poured concrete walls have an integral yellow pigment, and are bush-hammered to bring out the texture of the aggregate.

You can glimpse the winemaking process and look down on the lower-level loading area before exploring the interior. A curved barrier encircles the reception desk. From here a narrow ramp coils down between an inner wall of gabions containing river rocks and a retaining wall of poured concrete. Halfway down, the inner wall is cut away to provide an overview of the sunken oval barrel room with its slender concrete structural columns supporting a bowed cove-lit wood ceiling. There's a great sense of mystery as you spiral down into the earth and chance upon this glowing cave, with its floor-mounted pin spots casting long shadows across the gabions. One hopes the owners realize the potential for a choral music concert in this magical room. Beyond is a courtyard with a fountain to re-establish your relationship with the sky.

Odfjell designed his own winery and guest lodge (see page TK) and two others before putting architecture aside to return to his Norwegian family's container shipping business. One hopes he'll find time to do another, for his skill as an oenophile gives him unique insights into a winemaker's needs.

Visits by appointment. Tel: +56 032 741 500. Fundo El Rosario, Casablanca.
www.mateticvineyards.com

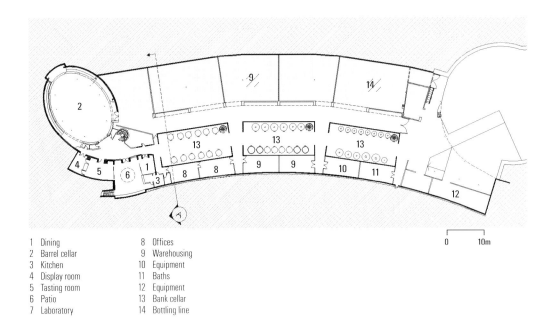

1 Dining
2 Barrel cellar
3 Kitchen
4 Display room
5 Tasting room
6 Patio
7 Laboratory
8 Offices
9 Warehousing
10 Equipment
11 Baths
12 Equipment
13 Bank cellar
14 Bottling line

0   10m

BODEGA SALENTEIN

Eliana Bormida and Mario Yanzón have practised architecture in Mendoza for 30 years and early on became interested in viticulture. They remodeled existing facilities and built their first ground-up winery in 1997. They now have about nine projects in design or construction, mostly in the burgeoning wine country to the south of this agreeable provincial capital. "Wine is not a product of industry but of land," says Yanzon. "We try to experience nature deeply, expressing the spirit of the mountains, stony soils and a lack of water, the brightness of the sun and the clarity of the air; the shifts from heat to cold, and the changing seasons. Each site has its own features so all our wineries are different."

Salentein is 4000 feet up in the Alto Valle de Uco, which is rapidly becoming a major wine-growing area, thanks to the rocky alluvial soil, drip-irrigated from underground rivers, and an average snowfall of six inches. The owner is Mijndert Pon, a Dutch businessman who embraced the economic potential of Argentina in fruit, cattle, tourism and now, wine. In a philanthropic gesture, he set aside 125 acres of his estate as a nature preserve, established a foundation to promote literacy, and another to develop the culture of the valley, which has a population of about 100,000. An art collector, he invited artists to design his wine labels in the colors of the Andes.

Pon had no background in wine and worked through Carlos Puñenta, who comes from a winemaking family. He is the general manager (besides managing his own winery, close to Mendoza) and came up with the idea of a centralized space, from which the architects derived the cruciform plan. The owner criticized their first proposal for a theatrical entrance, asking that building be direct and simple, but then gave the architects complete freedom. They selected traditional brick, rough local stone, and tinted concrete floors for ease of construction.

Terraces planted with local grasses step up a rise to the pale brick building with its shallow-pitched corrugated tin roof, set against the backdrop of the mighty Andes. Trees extend from each wing of the Greek cross plan, which contains four wine-making operations, one in each wing. These include the Finca El Portillo and Salentein bottlings of Cabernet Sauvignon, Merlot and Malbec, and the Salentein Primus Pinot Noir. Small tanks are located at ground level and barrel rooms 27 feet below, opening onto a central amphitheater. Behind the reception desk in the elongated lobby there's a glimpse of the tank room with its high-tech steel roof and round opening that looks down into the barrel cellar.

"Nature here is so imposing that we decided to hollow out the earth and make people feel the darkness," says Bormida. Sun comes down through an opening in the roof and down to the center of the barrel room. This is a theater in the round with a circular stone-paved "stage" with an inset compass rose; barrels are set out on steps and stacked beneath round arches in the four stepped transepts. Steps leading to the tasting rooms are entered through a dramatically lit archway.

Since completing the 80,000-square-foot winery, Bormida & Yanzón have added an ecumenical chapel that expresses the spirit of the land in an intensely spiritual way. The walls are of rammed earth blocks, a traditional building technique that is brought up to date by threading rebar through the blocks and bracing them with concrete rings at the top and base. Steel roof trusses are also used to conform to the seismic code, but these are concealed by a bamboo ceiling. Narrow skylights, a baffled rear window, and small square openings to either side admit soft natural light. A second building has been added on the same central approach axis to house a visitors' center, restaurant, and art gallery, with an auditorium for the presentation of a video on the year-round cycle of nature. To round out the program for this destination winery, a new posada (bed and breakfast) will be constructed to replace the present modest building.

Tours by appointment. Tel: +54 261 423 8514. RP 89, Tunuyan, Mendoza. www.bodegasalentein.com

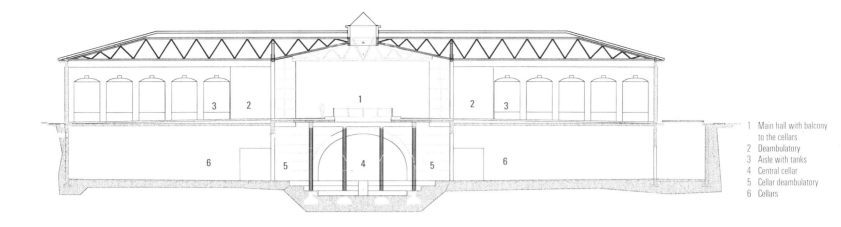

1 Main hall with balcony
  to the cellars
2 Deambulatory
3 Aisle with tanks
4 Central cellar
5 Cellar deambulatory
6 Cellars

STAG'S LEAP CELLARS

"Winemaking is a fusion of art and science, intuition and the senses, plus a rational process—and we tried to express that poetically," is how assistant winemaker Julia Winiarski explains the complex of cellars that were dug into the hill below her father's winery. They discovered that the rock was diorite—probably from the core of an extinct volcano—which made their task harder, but guaranteed that the tunnels would remain stable without reinforcement.

After rejecting a basic grid plan as too factory-like, they started playing with different lengths of tunnel to provide storage for fruit from different lots and curving them to achieve a sense of surprise and to reflect the natural curvature of the hill. Five tunnels converge on a circular area, the symbolic heart of the caves; a piazza at the center of the subterranean labyrinth. The goal was to create a sense of place—for visitors and the people who worked there—and climate-controlled storage for 6000 barrels. The caves have a constant temperature of 62 degrees Fahrenheit and humidity of 95 percent or higher—ideal for aging red wines. Fortuitously, the cellar plan also resembles that of Napa Valley, with its central river flanked by two highways that are linked by connector roads.

Warren Winiarski, who founded Stag's Leap Cellars, sought an architect to complete the project, and chose Javier Barba after seeing a photograph of the earth-rooted villa he designed for Lord Rothschild on Corfu. The Barcelona-based architect had built nothing in the United States, but he proved an ideal choice. Barba remembers his first glimpse of the excavation: "It looked like the entrance to an abandoned mine. It was a brutal space, but I loved it!" He designed an arcade of sloping concrete ribs clad in rammed earth that wrap around the hillside, linking two entries to the cave. They suggest flying buttresses supporting the exposed rock, which is stabilized by copper mesh and ornamental bosses wrapped over steel rods that are driven 20 feet into the ground. Winiarski was delighted. "You can see the rock crumbling, and bits of root from the trees growing above," he observes. "You can observe the process that creates our soil. I wanted this structure to tell that story, and it does."

Barba created a Great Room, with a kitchen, for entertaining, sealed off at either end with massive, hand-crafted redwood doors. The room is separated from the caves as a museum lobby is separated from the art galleries, to preserve the integrity of both. It's paved with quartzite and the barrel vault and walls are sprayed with Shotcrete and plastered with flecks of feldspar to give them a sparkle. The room is lit from wall sconces: pierced copper cones that suggest bubbles rising in a champagne glass. Rock erupts from one corner of the room.

Beyond, a curved tunnel leads to the rotunda, where Barba has used the same materials and lighting. A Foucault pendulum shows that the earth is rotating on its axis. "We think of this as the beating heart of our cave and the movement is a metaphor for the passing of time and aging of our wines," says Winiarski. Barba has strengthened that reference to the earth turning

by bowing the quartzite pavement, whose pattern suggests a patchwork of fields seen from above, and creating the illusion of a star-filled sky. He went on to design another earth-rooted structure: a new visitors' center that is rooted in the other side of the hill from his arcade, and takes its cue from a rock outcrop on the far side of the valley.

Winiarski reflects on what he has achieved over the past four decades. "The crushing of the grapes marks a moment of consummation: the grapes die and the wine is born," he muses. "The arcade gave importance to that role. A winery should reveal itself slowly, like going through the skins of an onion. When we started, in the 1960s, the growth in the size and quality of Napa wineries could not have been foreseen. The moment of realization came when we won top prize in the Franco–American tasting of 1976, the 200th anniversary of Jefferson's first vinicultural endeavor."

Open daily. Tours by reservation. Tel: +1 707 944 2020. 5788 Silverado Trail, Napa, California. www.cask23.com

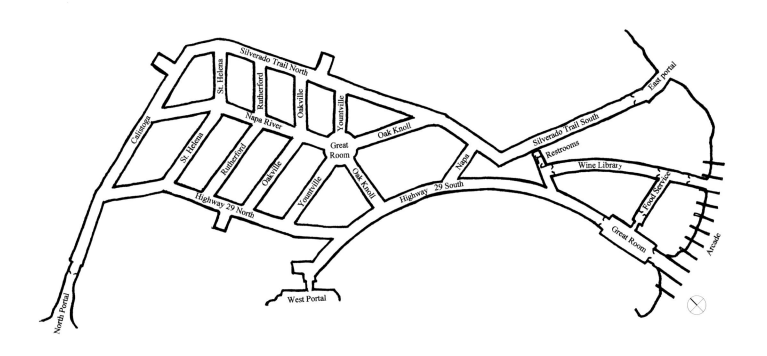

QUINTESSA

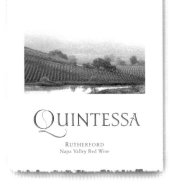

Valeria Huneeus, who has a doctorate in microbiology and a passion for everything that grows, outmaneuvered other suitors for a 280-acre estate in the prestigious Rutherford district. Incredibly, the estate had never been farmed, and she introduced high-density planting, varied root stocks, clonal grafts, vertical trellising and other innovative ideas. She and her husband, Agustin, a fellow Chilean and veteran vintner, christened their property Quintessa—for its five hills and also in the hope they could develop a premium red of quintessential excellence. In the nine years since they released their first vintage, a blend of selected Cabernet Sauvignon, Merlot, and Cabernet Franc, they've fulfilled their goal, and they now have a handsome new winery in which they, and winemaker Sarah Gott, can make further improvements.

The owners wanted an inconspicuous structure of simple materials that would blend into the hillside, minimizing the impact of the building on existing vineyards and landscape and employing a gentle, gravity flow system of handling the grapes. "Wine is a statement of place," declared Agustin Huneeus, and he chose Walker Warner Architects, a San Francisco partnership, for their sensitivity to this issue, even though they had never before designed a winery. The architects embedded the production areas within a hillside, facing what they called "a natural amphitheater" with a crescent wall of local tufa, mixed with stone from Texas and northern California to pick up on colors in the landscape. The stone arc faces northeast toward the Silverado Trail, and it has a symbolic central portal—steel-framed glass doors that pull natural light into the tank room.

Ramps lead up from either side, and the roof of the winery doubles as the crush pad. Grapes are sorted, funneled through ports and a movable chute to French oak fermentation tanks in the production hall below. These can be accessed from a mezzanine gallery which supports the glass-walled office and lab—the winemaker's command post. The grapes are crushed in a basket press, transferred to barrels, and aged in caves that extend back into hillside for a total of 1200 feet and can be entered through four porticoes to the rear of the production hall. Huneeus set the capacity at 75,000 cases, far in excess of the current annual production of 10,000.

To the rear of the crush deck is a stone-walled central pavilion, lit from a clerestory, and flanked by low office wings in steel-framed glass that are shaded with wood slats and a projecting roof plane. The environmentally conscious design, which includes an irrigated sod roof, thermal mass, and the use of night air ventilation, minimizes the need for heating and cooling. A lofty reception area is furnished as a living room with chairs drawn up to an open fire. Behind this is a warm, intimate tasting/sales room with a steel grid of cork ceiling soffits, stone walls at front and back, poured concrete at the sides, and a polished brown concrete floor with an exposed aggregate. Torcheres are clamped to elegant cruciform steel columns, and the wine shelves and bar are made of stacked black walnut. Backlit vellum paintings symbolize the seasons. Natural light spills down around the ceiling soffits onto a stone wall with gridded wood doors leading into the vaulted VIP tasting room, which hints at the caves below. These have a grid plan with a rotunda, marked by an obelisk fountain, and the tunnel leading to this may be used as an art gallery without compromising the temperature and humidity levels of the other caves.

Open daily. Tours by appointment. Tel: +1 707 967 1601. 1601 Silverado Trail, St Helena, California. www.quintessa.com

1 Fermentation room
2 Crush terrace
3 Technical tasting room
4 Winemaking laboratory
5 Lobby pavilion
6 Visitor tasting room
7 Visitor tasting cave
8 Barrel caves
9 Central cave rotunda

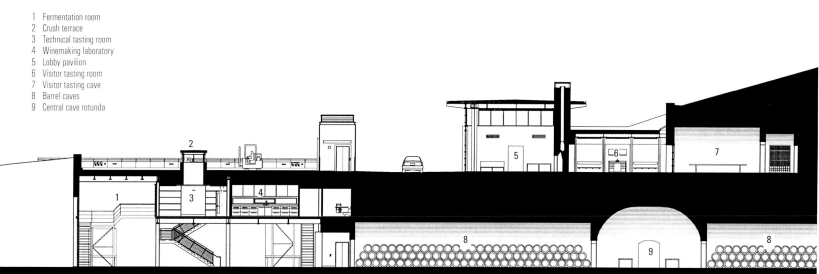

0   20m

CANTINA GHIDOSSI

CADENAZZO, SWITZERLAND
Aurelio Galfetti, 2002

Gianfranco Ghidossi is an electrical engineer, living and working in a small apartment building he designed in Bellinzona, the tiny capital of Ticino canton. His father made *vin ordinaire*, as is common in this farming region; the son resolved to improve on this by making small quantities of premium wine. He bought a five-acre plot on a steep slope just outside the town, and planted it with Chardonnay and Merlot grapes. A funicular leads up through the first block of vines, planted in serried rows, to a rocky bluff; the second tier rises from there.

For the design of the winery, Ghidossi turned to Aurelio Galfetti, a friend and one of a talented group of Italian and Swiss architects who have made the Ticino Valley a center of rationalist architecture. Their work is distinguished by its simple forms and materials, a lack of pretension, and a quiet, humane poetry—exactly the qualities an engineer most appreciates. Galfetti produced a triumph of minimalism that engages the landscape: a two-story concrete box built into the hillside, just above the road. Production activities are located at the lower level, and exterior stairs lead up to the shady roof terrace, from where you can gaze back to the town and the medieval fortress that Galfetti restored.

Visitors drive to the upper level, and enter a long reception room. At one end is a kitchen with a window framing a view of town and its signature castle to the east. Side walls are lined with bottles in climate-controlled vitrines. At the west end, glass sliders open up to a paved terrace, separated from the vines by a dry-stone wall.

Galfetti offered a few observations on his modest modern farm building: "With today's electronic systems, wine-producing conditions are as good as, if not better than, those of the old wineries. What can our times add to the two rows of aluminum and glass cupboards, one for reds and the other for whites? Quite a lot, actually. A table big enough to enjoy people's company among the bottles; two large glass walls offering beautiful views over the vineyard and the countryside away in the distance (cozily warm in winter and refreshingly cool in winter); and two walls and a concrete roof to round everything off. What place does nostalgia have here? It is found in the wisteria-draped steel pergola that covers the concrete and the glass, making the light softer, and taking some of the sharpness from the aluminum window frames, while the machine-finished local stone floor and the wooden table transport us back to another age."

Not open to the public. info@galfetti.com

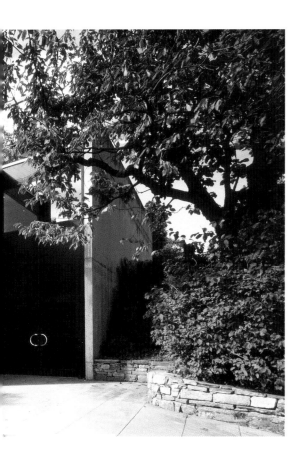

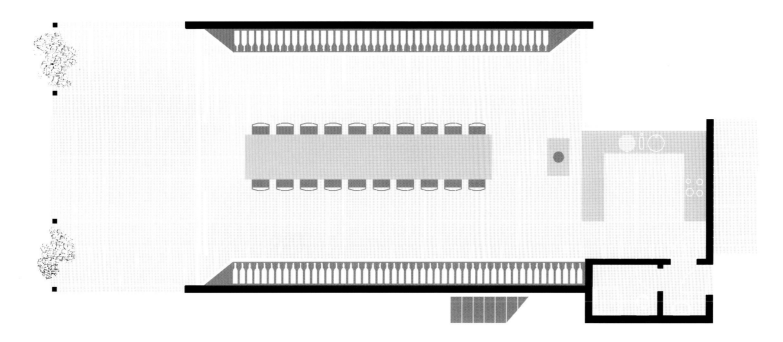

TARRAWARRA MUSEUM OF ART AND TASTING ROOM

YARRA VALLEY, VICTORIA, AUSTRALIA

Allan Powell Architects, 2002–2003

Architecture as art, an hour's drive north of Melbourne. Winemakers Marc and Eva Besen wanted to share the distinguished collection of modern Australian art they've been building since the late 1950s, so they leased a site to the State Government for 99 years, commissioned a museum to house 140 art works and funded its upkeep. In doing so, they created a major cultural resource for the Yarra Valley, and provided a bonus for visiting oenophiles. Allan Powell won the competition with a design that he likens to an earthwork for the way that it mediates between the protected interiors and the dramatic landscape. Gently curved walls enclose four lofty galleries that are rooted in the hillside. At the south end, a huge shutter slides back to frame a stunning vista of the sloping vineyard and distant hills. A curved translucent glass prow (the lobby below, an office above) faces an elliptical restaurant/tasting room across a walled courtyard that is punctuated by eight slender concrete monoliths.

The walls of the restaurant catch the light, and the shadow patterns of the pergola that extends down the outer side. Openings in the wall along the east terrace frame fragments of the vineyard. The earthy character of the exterior is carried inside with the concrete aggregate floor and exposed rammed earth walls. The design draws strength and inspiration from these rough textures. A lunch of plump Tasmanian oysters with opal basil and sherry granita, and boudin blanc with a salad of apple, celery and rocket, accompanied by Chardonnay and Pinot Noir was the perfect sequel to a morning exploring the work of unfamiliar painters. TarraWarra demonstrates how Australians have embraced the good life and found a novel architectural expression for art, food, and wine.

Winery open daily; museum open Thursday–Sunday. Tel: +61 3 5962 3311.
311 Healesville Road, Yarra Glen, Victoria. www.tarrawarra.com.au

1 Drop off area
2 Entry
3 Walkway
4 Central courtyard
5 Cafe/wine tasting
6 Service yard
7 Kitchen
8 Wine store/sales
9 Male toilets
10 Disabled toilets
11 Baby change
12 Utility
13 Female toilets
14 Service cupboard
15 Entry walkway
16 Reception
17 Offices
18 Exit walkway
19 South gallery
20 Gallery
21 North gallery
22 Vista walk

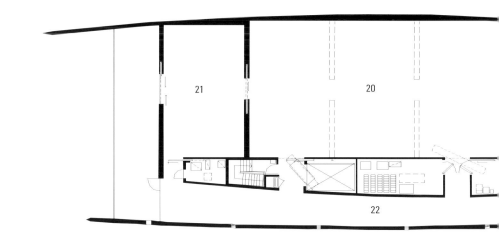

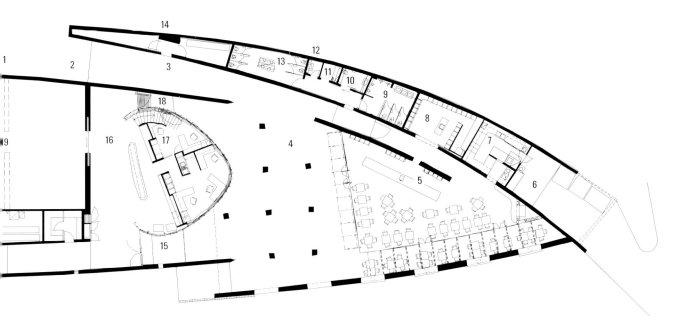

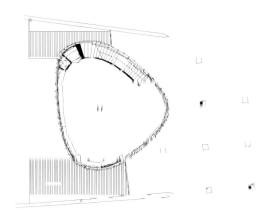

MONUMENTAL PRESENCE

ARGENTINA

AUSTRALIA

SPAIN

USA

CANADA

BODEGA SEPTIMA

Septima, named for the lucky number in Latin American cultures, is the first Argentinian property of the Spanish wine group Codorníu. They bought a 750-acre estate, half of which is planted with Malbec, Syrah, Cabernet Sauvignon and Tempranillo, and commissioned Bormida & Yanzón to design a winery with a strong regional identity, production on a single level, and generous spaces for hospitality. A massive stone block, as impassive and powerful as an ancient temple, rises from a 3500-foot-high plateau just off the highway that leads from Mendoza, over the dizzying heights of the Andes to Santiago.

The architects were inspired by the traditional *pircas* (piled rock walls) of the Huarpes people. Here, the rough, locally quarried stones are layered in four courses of diminishing size with a stone rib between each and are set into reinforced concrete with deep foundations to resist earthquakes. The rocks were locally quarried and the exposed concrete is earth-toned. Walls are more than three feet thick to provide good thermal insulation. The drama of the mass is enhanced by the backdrop of mountains, which are snow covered from July through November. The building is set back 500 yards from the highway, with an axial drive to come. Tinted glass cuts glare from the northern sun on the projecting hospitality bay; the rest of the 440-foot-long façade is windowless. Native grasses soften the hard edges, and concrete steps lead up from either side of the entry to a central terrace above the barrel room.

The long lobby has hardwood floors and screens to mask the tasting room at one end, and offices at the other. A lighting strip is clad in a band of perforated metal, and tall windows frame the barrel room behind the reception desk. As at Pérez Cruz and Dominus, there is a linear flow from one end of the building to the other. Grapes are sorted and loaded into fermentation tanks to the east, and cases (there is capacity for up to 100,000) are shipped from the west. A steel gallery carries visitors over the tanks and barrels, to the bottling line and storage (separated by a glass-walled lab). The second-level reception room opens onto the central and west terraces. Nothing could be simpler or more appropriate, in organization and in the powerful impression Septima makes on visitors.

Tours Monday–Friday, by appointment. Tel: +54 261 498 5164. Ruta Internacional No. 7, Km 6.5, Agrelo, Lujan de Cuyo. www.bodegaseptima.com.at

SHADOWFAX WINERY

WERRIBEE, VICTORIA, AUSTRALIA

Wood Marsh, 1999–2001

A thirty-minute drive southwest from Melbourne, this premium winery was developed by a consortium of wine experts on a wooded site adjoining the landmark 19th-century Werribee Mansion, which is now an exclusive restaurant and hotel, but open for tours. The winery is named for Gandalf's horse in *The Lord of the Rings*—a prescient choice, given the overwhelming popularity of the movie adaptation of Tolkien's trilogy.

Because it's a heritage site, the new building had to be reticent, and so it was designed to resemble an earthwork (with a nod to American artist Michael Heizer) in the form of a truncated pyramid. There are four linked bays, clad in CorTen (self-rusting steel) containing the lofty cellar door, barrel room and lab, tanks, bottling and storage, with a capacity of 20,000 cases a year. Fork lifts can drive through glass sliders between each bay. Lattice sun shades are wrapped around an upper story of glass-fronted offices at the north end, and a red stair spiraling around an elevator leads up to these, and down to the underground barrel cellar.

As in other Australian and New Zealand wineries, there's a big emphasis on cellar-door sales, and a full bay is devoted to a casual restaurant, display, and a long tasting bar that's backed by angular panels of colored glass. It would be a pity to deny yourself the pleasure of sampling the powerful (though pricey) Shiraz, or the distinctive Chardonnay, Pinot Gris, and Pinot Noir offerings. This diversity of varietals and blends is made possible by shipping fruit in tankers from distant vineyards—another distinctively Australian practice.

Even when Shadowfax has closed for the day, it's worth driving out to admire it as a sculptural object. In the late afternoon, there's a wonderful play of sunlight and shadows off the rich brown surfaces; light reaches in through glass to illuminate barrels, and the production areas can be glimpsed from one end to the other. From the sides, you are reminded   as the architects doubtlessly intended—of ancient pyramids, suggesting an affinity between this structure and the primitive massing of Dominus.

Open daily. Tel: +61 3 9731 4420. K Road, Werribee, Victoria. www.shadowfax.com.au

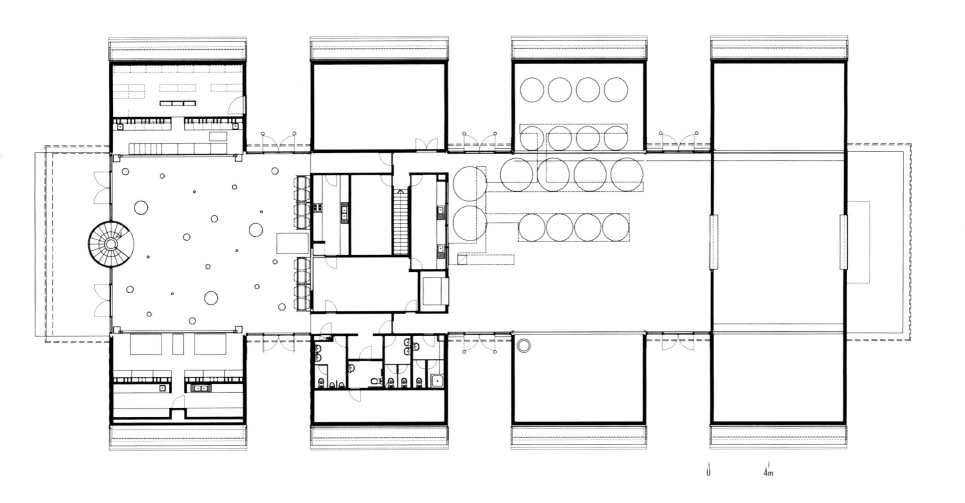

LEGARIS

RIBERA DE DUERO, SPAIN

Domingo Triay, 1999–2001

The latest venture of the Codorníu Group is dedicated to the production of quality red wine from a 230-acre estate planted with Tempranillo and Pinot Noir grapes in Ribera del Duero, a region that is challenging the preeminence of La Rioja to the northeast. Legaris ("you shall be harvested" in Latin) was designed by a Barcelona-based architect who was responsible for three earlier properties of the group. In contrast to his fellow Catalonian, Santiago Calatrava, Triay is a rationalist and his buildings are deceptively simple. In this 82,000-square-foot structure he economized by using industrial materials to build four plain sheds divided by a concourse linking the production areas, and a cross axis leading from entry to offices. As the architect observes: "The exterior is deliberately hermetic and inexpensive—a minimal, neutral container. As with a bottle of wine, the surprise should always lurk within."

An airy portico, orientation theater, and light-filled lobby are rotated 45 degrees to the main building to emphasize the entry. A red pergola contrasts vividly with the soft yellow cladding panels. A tasting room with ceramic walls and four tall tables flows out of the reception area. The courtyard evokes the cloister of a monastery, but its raked white gravel suggests a dry zen garden.

Red pergolas to either side are reflected in the polished floors of the second-story concourse. From this upper level, visitors can look down into the production areas as they pass the elegant glass display screens with their integrated steel lighting fixtures. The interior is infused with a spirit of tranquility: windows at the end of each concourse frame views of the vineyards and, to the south, the fairytale castle of Peñafiel perched on its hilltop. The wine library is the one tightly enclosed space: a wood-lined cube with a mezzanine gallery, central table, cabinets and racks under the steps.

"An architect must create spaces where wines can live," says Triay. "There's a common association between old buildings and the aging of wine, so visitors are unaccustomed to contemporary buildings. At the beginning of the 21st century, we have to create a new iconography." That opinion is echoed by the winemaker, Berta Laguna. "We have to be open to new ways of making wine," she explains. "The goal is to reconcile tradition and technology, and this winery is in the middle of that."

Visits by appointment. Tel: +34 983 878 088. Ctra. Peñafiel-Encinas de Esgueva, Curiel de Duero. www.legaris.com

OPUS ONE

"More landscape than architectural statement," is how Scott Johnson describes the premium winery he designed for a joint venture by the Mondavis of Napa and the Rothschilds of Bordeaux. Its elliptical façade emerges from a grassy berm, conveying a sense of mystery and quiet grandeur. The symbolism is apt. This low-profile mix of tradition and technology is home to one of the world's great wines.

The project was born of a short meeting in 1978. Baron Philippe de Rothschild had recently won a fifty-year battle to secure First Growth classification for Chateau Mouton Rothschild. Robert Mondavi had travelled the world in search of techniques that would make his winery a pace-setter among California's producers. The two visionaries agreed to pool their ideas and resources to create a Bordeaux-style premium wine in the Napa Valley. Reactions to the announcement were mixed, but skeptics were won over as soon as the first vintage was released from the Robert Mondavi winery in 1984, and the two partners felt justified in commissioning a new building.

Four firms were invited to submit proposals; Johnson Fain and Pereira Associates of Los Angeles won the approval of the two families. Design Partner Scott Johnson and colleagues spent three days and nights sketching a building that could be read as the portico to a cellar, or as a building that the ground rose to embrace. "I liked the ambiguity and the way the building explains itself as you get into it," remarks Johnson. The clients approved its understated originality, so different from the Mission-style Mondavi winery across the road, or the Rothschilds' stone farmhouse.

Five years elapsed before construction began. The first design proved too large and costly, and had to be scaled down; a high water table and hot springs were discovered on the site; and the first priority was to replant the 100-acre vineyard. "Initially, the French were afraid it would look too American, and the Americans had the opposite fear," he recalls. "We even developed a radically different concept to test their commitment to the first design." The clients didn't waver, and the two cultures achieved a satisfying equilibrium. As built, the 70,000-square-foot winery has a production capacity of up to 30,000 cases.

The boldly modeled walls of smooth and rusticated limestone and the central rotunda evoke the revolutionary French architect, Claude-Nicholas Ledoux. But the neo-classical formality is softened by the grass-covered berm from which the cornice emerges as an abstract sculptural form. A gentle ramp leads up to the landscaped semicircle of the entrance courtyard. Grass and stone, olives and cloisters: the associations are timeless and universal. The rotunda serves as entrance and hub. Stairs and an elevator lead down to the lower level and up to the roof terrace. Sunlight filters through a redwood pergola and glass pyramid to cast its dappled shadows across the smoothly plastered walls. A barrel-vaulted reception room opens off to the left.

There's a dramatic transition from the light-filled reception areas, with their eclectic furnishings and refined detailing, to the shadowy working areas with their concrete block walls. For the winemakers, these areas have their own poetry. The vineyard is divided into 40 plots, and the character of each

is determined by geology, microclimate and the degree of slope, which affects drainage. Grapes are brought to the long space behind the salon in small baskets to be hand-sorted on mobile conveyor belts and crushed. The pulp is gravity-fed to big stainless-steel tanks in the space below. Later, the fledgling wine is siphoned into new oak barrels, up to a thousand of which are arranged in a single layer within the curved fermenting room. Here the wine is topped and fined with egg whites until it is moved to another area for aging, making room for the next vintage.

Expansive windows in the tasting room frame a dramatic vista of the barrels curving away into darkness, a spectacle to delight architects and oenophiles in equal measure. "For me, architecture is about room-making, circulation, and the play of light," says Johnson. "The curves—in the rotunda, the forecourt, the barrel vault and cellar—carry associations of timelessness and longevity, while evoking the process of making and savoring wine, from tank to barrel, and bottle to glass."

Tours by appointment. Tel: + 1 707 944 9442. 7900 St Helena Highway, Oakville, California. www.opusonewinery.com

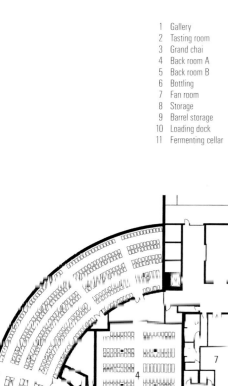

1 Gallery
2 Tasting room
3 Grand chai
4 Back room A
5 Back room B
6 Bottling
7 Fan room
8 Storage
9 Barrel storage
10 Loading dock
11 Fermenting cellar

1 Courtyard
2 Gate house
3 Reception area
4 Tasting room
5 Public relations office
6 Laboratory
7 Conference room
8 Offices
9 Floral prep area
10 Kitchen
11 Storage area
12 Tank access platform

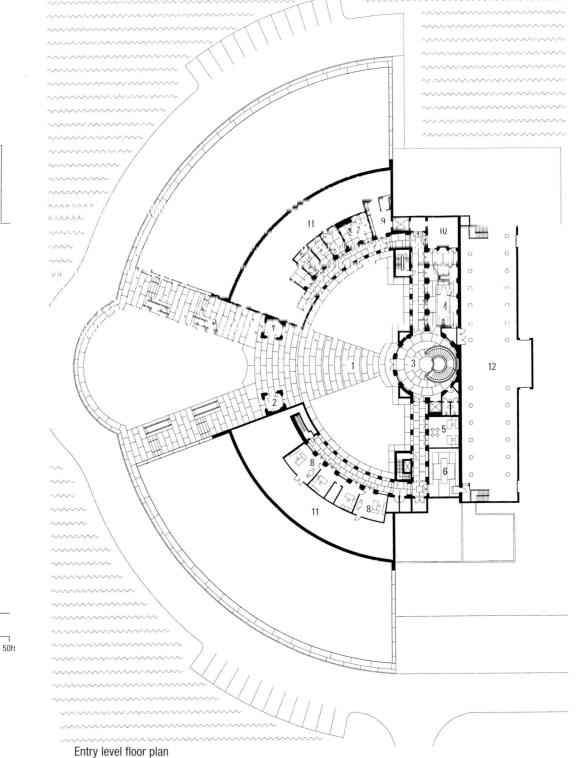

Lower level floor plan

0   50ft

Entry level floor plan

MISSION HILL FAMILY ESTATE

OKANAGAN VALLEY, CANADA

Olson Sundberg Kundig Allen Architects, 2000–2002

Like Opus One, this ambitious premium winery is a modernist riff on classical architecture, a fusion of Old World tradition and New World innovation. The owner, Anthony von Mandl, was born in Vancouver, but his father is Viennese and he grew up in central Europe. "Wine and food were my parents' way of life, and, having worked as an importer, I wanted to make my own wine," he says. "Early on, I dreamed of a winery with underground cellars, anchored by a bell tower, overlooking a lake and orchards that reminded me of northern Italy."

He discovered the Okanagan Valley, part of a 300-mile-long strip of desert and finger lakes protected by the Coastal and Monashee mountains, extending north from the US–Canadian border. Like the desert valleys of central Chile, it produces what he calls "amazing fruit," but it was mostly going into jug wine when he bought a rustic, run-down winery in 1981. He put up new buildings, brought in winemaker John Simes from New Zealand, and chef Michael Allemeir from South Africa during his long struggle to win respect for his product. His goal was to produce up to 300,000 cases a year and to create a destination that would focus attention on the Valley.

To create buildings that would express his vision, he chose Tom Kundig, a partner in Seattle's leading architectural firm, for his mastery of the contemporary idiom and classical proportions. The product of their discussions and visits to wineries in Napa and Europe, was a complex of buildings that have the mass and timelessness of a monastery. A broken arch leads to a grassy courtyard that becomes an amphitheater at one corner, sloping down to a view over the vines and lake. That vista is framed by two loggias, a reception hall and the campanile, with the ivy-clad façade of the old winery to the right. Poured shuttered concrete alternates with yellow-toned precast concrete and stone trim. It's a stage for public activities: a place for picnicking on the grass or enjoying alfresco Shakespeare; dining beneath one loggia and lingering in another while waiting for a tour, or buying a case or a corkscrew in the store. Semi-private, glass walled tasting rooms open out of the store and provide a glimpse of barrels stacked on massive wood frame. In contrast to most wineries, Mission Hill has atmospheric lighting that gives it a new life after dark.

The winery comprises 140,000 square feet and nearly all the production areas are located below the public spaces, and concealed within the hillside. The two levels are interwoven. The 108-foot tower serves as a symbolic link from earth to sky, and is ingeniously constructed as a self-supporting spiral of precast concrete panels. Tours start in the chapel-like hall, with its barrel vault, triangular limestone pavers, and deep-set slot windows that protect a large Chagall tapestry from direct sun. This is a Bacchanalian scene in rich, dark colors, woven in France under the artist's supervision in 1991, shortly before his death. Behind the end wall is a small theater for the introductory

video, which opens up to a kitchen for cookery classes and catering to invited guests—including a recent conference of Western premiers.

Steps lead down to a barrel cellar blasted out of volcanic rock beneath the reception hall; poured concrete arches and a vortex drain beneath the bell tower to carry away rain water. Rare wines are stacked behind a locked gate; amphorae dating back to 2800 BC are displayed on a back wall. A private tasting area and dining room beneath the loggia open out of the barrel cellar; the long table is set off by Gothic gilt torcheres and a Fernand Leger tapestry. Outside is an Austrian baroque fountain of circa 1636, which, like the heraldic emblem of a pelican plucking its breast on the entry arch, reminds you of the owner's deep roots in Europe.

"Robert Mondavi was my mentor. I want to put Okanagan on the map as he did with Napa, and give visitors an experience they will remember for the rest of their lives," says Mandl. "It had to take them out of the quotidian world, to a place that's tranquil and contemplative, where they can recognize the art of fine wine making."

Open daily. Group reservations. Tel: +1 250 768 6448.
1730 Mission Hill Road, Westbank, British Columbia.
www.missionhillwinery.com

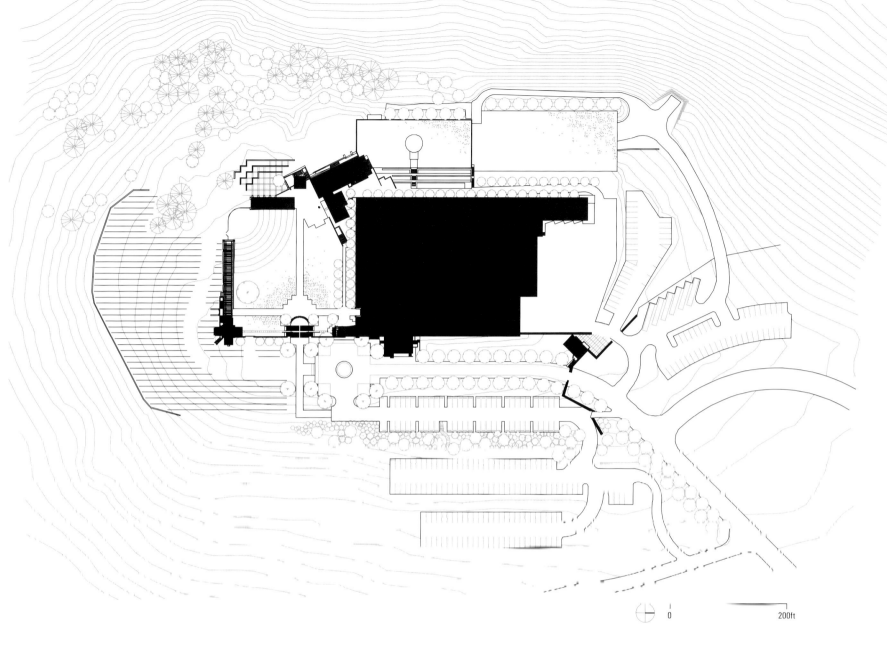

RAVENTOS I BLANC

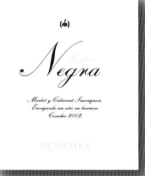

Miguel Raventos founded a winery in Catalonia in 1681, and in the 1870s his descendants produced the first Spanish cava —a sparking wine that is made using the same method as Champagne, and which has won a succession of awards for this family firm. To establish a new identity, they sold their hundred-year-old house and winery—an art nouveau masterpiece by Puig i Cadafalch—to Codorníu, moved to the adjoining 250-acre estate, and commissioned a modern winery from the Barcelona architects Jaume Bach and Gabriel Mora.

Inspired by barns and the functional tradition of early factories, the architects have created a complex that is simple but grand, a synthesis of agriculture and industry with a timeless beauty. Red bricks and tiles are used throughout to add warmth to the rigorous geometry of the buildings, and the elegant steel porches and sliding gates. An elliptical reception area with a polished marble floor and pale green Venetian stucco walls leads to meeting rooms and upstairs offices. The arcade on the inner side flows into a line of brick pillars that form a circular enclosure around a huge and ancient oak.

Grapes are taken to a raised courtyard, where—at the base of a tower that serves as a belvedere—they are gravity fed into presses. From there, the juice is conveyed to the production building, a grand arched space with a springy ceiling vault that is lit from three tiers of gables and rounded openings facing north to the peak of Monserrat. The cava is aged in bottles in a long barrel-vaulted cellar that can accommodate an annual production of 60,000 cases a year, stored in V-shaped racks and constantly rotated. The dramatically lit tunnel extends back to a tasting room with a rear wall that is curved around the roots of the oak.

Tours by appointment. Tel: +34 93 891 0602. Placa del Roure, Sant Sadurni d'Anoia. www.raventos.com

RURAL VERNACULAR

CHILE

AUSTRALIA

SPAIN

USA

NEW ZEALAND

BODEGA EN LOS ROBLES

COLCHAGUA VALLEY, CHILE

José Cruz Ovalle with Hernán Cruz & Ana Turell, 2000–2002

Chile's first organic winery is located six miles from the highway down a stony track with no signage. Getting there is an adventure that is amply rewarded by buildings that have a rich earthiness, in their massing, textures, and details. The architects have employed adobe blocks, wood beams and slats in conjunction with a reinforced concrete foundation that should withstand earthquakes. They've abstracted the rural vernacular, marrying old and new in a harmonious ensemble. It's a farmer's heavy jacket beside the tailored suit of Viña Pérez Cruz. And it expresses the organic character of the product as well as the earlier structure dramatizes the refinement of its wine.

Six production buildings were planned. The four that have been completed in the first phase are similar in form and are set at slight angles to each other to define an axis that leads the eye to the storage building and manager's office, 300 yards away across the vineyard. Each has a split pitched roof with a south-facing clerestory, a wood-frame structure with angled beams set on concrete posts supporting the roof and a canted wood grille above bowed infill walls of adobe blocks atop a base of rocks set in concrete — what Frank Lloyd Wright called "desert masonry" when he first used it at Taliesin West. A rough stone pavement and a dry-stone wall extend the buildings into the landscape. The ends of each block and a range of offices down the side of one tank room are faced with plain wood siding, and a wood stair spirals up to a gallery above the tanks. The two remaining buildings should be completed by 2008.

Visits by appointment. Tel: +56 2 353 9130.   www.vinedosemiliana.cl

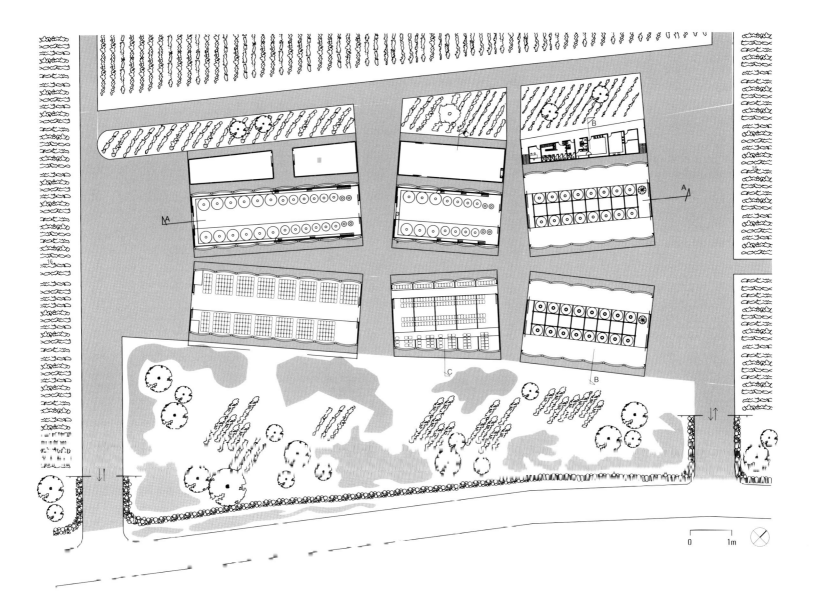

LERIDA ESTATE

LAKE GEORGE REGION, NSW, AUSTRALIA

Glenn Murcutt, 2002–2003

When Jim Lumbers retired from management consulting, he recalled a life-long interest in wine, drew on his expertise in microbiology, and bought a vineyard in the Lake George region, 30 miles from Canberra. Cold nights and deep alluvial soil promised plenty of flavor and aroma in the fruit. Lumbers' goal was to make up to 5000 cases of premium Pinot Gris and Pinot Noir, selling most of his output at the cellar door and the balance to restaurants. After talking to several architects, he wrote to Glenn Murcutt, a brilliant maverick who works alone and won the Pritzker Architecture Prize in 2002. "I wanted to complement a special site and I was inspired by wineries I remembered visiting as a kid, where you had to dodge the hoses and barrels," he says. "I wanted this to be an inside-out affair, with no barriers between hospitality and craft."

That program resonated with Murcutt. It was the architect's first winery, and he went directly to the basics. "Winemaking is a very industrial process, though it's often tarted up to look like something else," he observes. "Water is a major issue and, on this site, where there's no piped supply and rainfall is limited, we have to collect and store it ourselves." His search for the simplest way dictated the major features of the design. The broad, deeply corrugated shed roof is a self-supporting structure that drains into a row of water tanks lined up on the side facing the highway. The canopy is 20 feet high on the inner side to accommodate the fermentation tanks and a catwalk from which a plunger runs along a track to press the red wine grapes in open tanks. The water tanks block sun from the east and keep the interior cool, and the void beneath the canopy is shaded by tautly stretched red fabric panels.

The grapes are loaded to the north and follow a straight path to the retail outlet at the south end. Glass sliders divide the central barrel room from the spaces to either side, and concrete walls and a narrow clerestory maintain an even temperature and humidity. Visitors approach through the vines on a path of railroad ties, glimpsing the production areas before arriving at the cellar door. Expansive steel-framed windows frame a view over the valley and distant lake, and inwards to a walled courtyard with offices, a kitchen and lab to the rear. As Murcutt observes, "my ideal is to have a tasting area that's a part of the production, where you can enjoy the food and wine while smelling the casks. It's like an open kitchen in a restaurant, and gives the operation a sense of honesty and cleanliness."

Speeding along the federal highway from Canberra or Sydney, it's easy to miss Lerida. From afar, it looks almost generic, but as soon as you get close you realize how the architect has taken familiar forms and materials to achieve a kind of industrial poetry. The play of light off the corrugated tanks, the warm glow of the awnings, and the jagged edge of the roof heighten anticipation for what lies beyond, and provide just the right amount of enclosure and protection. Now, Lumbers is waiting to start on the house Murcutt will design for a site on the slope above the winery.

Open daily. Tel: +61 2 6295 6640. Old Federal Highway, Collector, New South Wales. www.leridaestate.com

BODEGAS JULIÁN CHIVITE

Señorío de Arínzano, Navarre, Spain

Rafael Moneo, 1998–2002

"From fathers to sons since 1647," is the Chivite motto, and four 11th-generation descendants of the family's first winegrower administer its latest acquisition, the 750-acre Señorío de Arínzano estate. It's a spectacular property, dominated by the Montejurra peak and straddling the Ega river, which flows from the Pyrenees to the Ebro. Chivite produces a third of the wine in the province of Navarre; for its premium brand, Colección 125, it commissioned a new winery from Rafael Moneo, who was born only 50 miles away, and is now Spain's most honored architect.

Moneo shared the client's respect for the land and its heritage, and the winery announces its presence to the road with nothing more than a concrete arch that frames Montejurra. An unpaved track leads through the vineyard and across the river to a spacious forecourt, where the new buildings embrace a patch of vines and three historic structures. Moneo is known for his austere exteriors, and his first winery is a model of restraint. Up to 19,000 cases a year can be produced in the 110,000 square feet of enclosed space, which is partly buried to minimize its bulk. The concrete walls are sandblasted to reveal a white pebbly aggregate that picks up on the color of the earth and should soon acquire the patina of stone. There are few openings and plastic pipes embedded in the concrete maintain an even temperature within during the rare extremes of heat and cold. The copper-clad roof should oxidize to match the holm oaks to the rear.

At Ysios and Legaris, the portico marks the public entrance; here the single architectural flourish of five projecting gables is to shade the grapes as they are unloaded. The bare concrete walls are a foil for a neo-classical chapel, a medieval tower that now serves as the caretaker's house, and an 18th-century manor house that Moneo remodeled to serve as a four-room inn for visitors.

As in his new Cathedral of Our Lady of the Angels in Los Angeles, Moneo has created an interior of great drama and beauty. A moving belt carries the grapes inside at the level of a catwalk from where they are fed into stainless steel tanks. The pitched pine vaults are set off by yellow stucco walls and a green concrete floor. The long, narrow barrel room is set at an 80-degree angle to the tank room, and is one of the architect's finest interiors. Slender beams fan from a row of stubby concrete columns, supporting the wide roof and a central walkway that carries visitors over the barrels. A pyramidal fermentation room, lit from a high window, serves as a hinge between these elongated rooms. The wine remains in the barrels for up to 24 months and then passes to a skylit bottling room and underground case storage. Another turn brings you to the tasting room, with its bay window framing the historic buildings. The old complements the new, which has already become an integral part of this fruitful land.

Open Monday–Friday, visits by appointment. Tel: +34 948 81 10 00. Ribera 34, 31592 Cintruénigo, Navarra. www.chivite.es

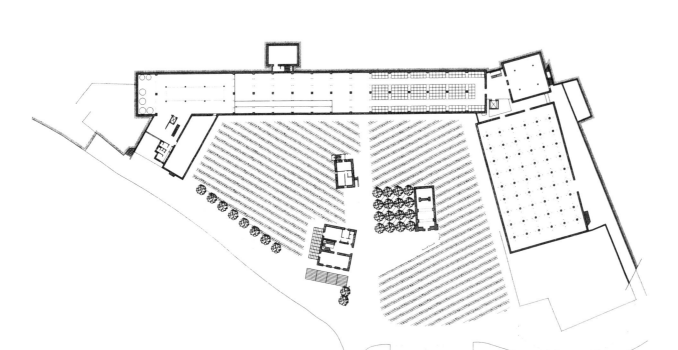

Upper level floor plan

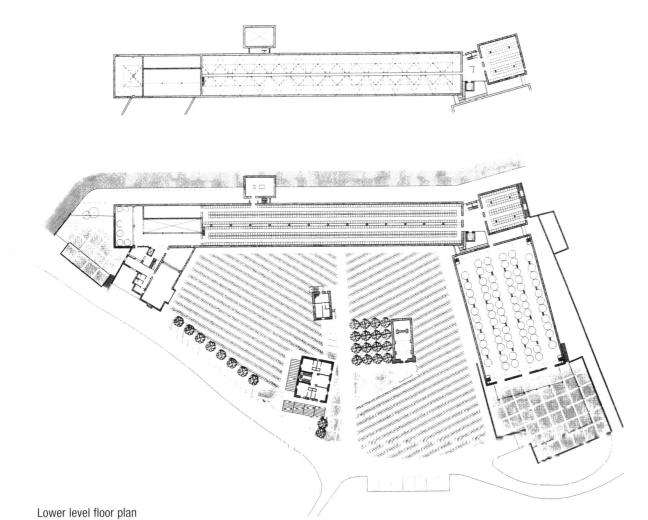

Lower level floor plan

BYRON

Cool ocean breezes flow into the Santa Maria Valley, to the north of Santa Barbara, making this an ideal region for Burgundian grape varieties. Ken Brown, a realtor turned winemaker, founded Byron in 1984 and rapidly acquired a reputation for his distinctive Pinot Noir, Chardonnay and Sauvignon Blanc varietals. When the Robert Mondavi family acquired the 125-acre estate in 1990, they promised Brown a new freedom to experiment, by enlarging the vineyard to 640 acres, and commissioning a new state-of-art winery with greatly increased capacity.

For architect Scott Johnson, it presented a congenial challenge, and a refreshing change of pace from the seven-year struggle to create Opus One for the Mondavi and Rothschild families in Napa Valley. Here, the client had a limited budget, clearly defined needs, and wanted the job done quickly. "The architecture wasn't such a big deal for them and that allowed me to deal with it in a more spontaneous way," Johnson explains. "When Byron came along we had been working on wineries for ten years, and softness of form was embedded in our minds. Landscape is a fabulous thing to me— I'm a country bumpkin really. I grew up in the Salinas Valley, surrounded by the soft folds of the hills that turn golden in summer. Here, in a similar setting, I thought how great it would be to design something that was minimalist and barely showed itself."

Johnson has realized that goal, while achieving much more. As you drive across the valley, you glimpse a graceful silver arc floating above the vineyards at the base of the bare hills. Gradually it emerges from the land as an abstraction of a barn, and finally it assumes the character of a rustic temple, with a grand portico supported on muscular, sharply angled beams. What was almost invisible from the edge of the vineyard, now has a commanding presence. The zinc-clad roof is a foil to the fir columns and cedar planks, earth tones and accents of bright color.

The entire 32,000-square-foot building, which has an annual capacity of 70,000 cases, was conceived as a production facility. It backs up to the hillside, allowing the grapes to be loaded at the upper level and gravity-fed into small, portable tanks. These are mounted on pneumatic jacks, so that they can easily be moved to the presses. Robert Mondavi has long pioneered new winemaking technologies, borrowing stainless steel tanks from the dairy industry in the 1960s, as well as electronic bottling systems from the soft drinks industry. Brown incorporated these innovations into the new winery and added his own refinements, which include four barrel rooms that can be kept at different temperatures and humidity levels.

Byron is more a lab than a factory, but its spaciousness and flexibility also make it a great place to entertain guests. Limited access delayed the introduction of public tours, making it unnecessary to build a visitors' center and tasting room in the first phase of construction. It's unlikely they will ever be needed, for the portico and the lofty hall leading out of it provide an ideal setting for receptions and a place for visitors to taste the wines. Large events are held in the fermentation room, where the tanks can be moved aside to clear the floor.

Visits by appointment. Tel: +1 805 937 7288. 5230 Tepusquet Road, Santa Maria, California. www.byronwines.com

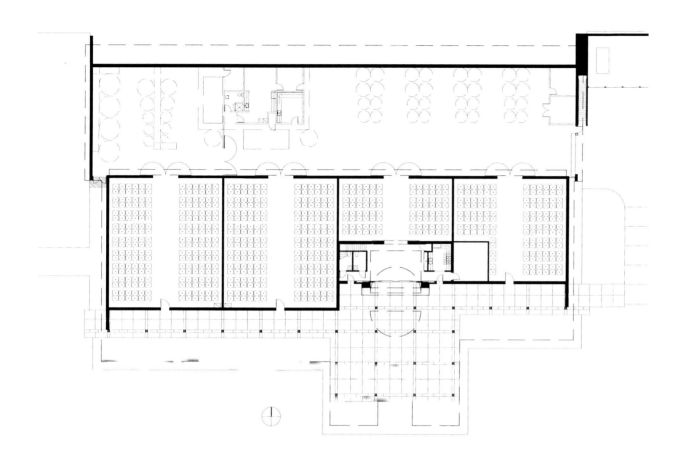

LONG MEADOW RANCH

Sequestered in the foothills of the Macayamas Mountains, this earthy facility is dedicated to the production of premium red wine and olive oil under the same roof—a first for the United States, though it is a common practice in Tuscany. It was conceived when owner Ted Hall invited his good friend William Turnbull—an architect with a fondness for barns and a passion for wine—to review his plans for the family farm. Hall wanted a tangible expression of his commitment to a high-quality, organic agricultural business, and to exploit the complementary growing seasons of grapes, which are usually harvested in September–October, and olives, which are gathered in December and January, allowing the ranch to operate efficiently year-round with a full-time crew.

Turnbull had already designed three Napa wineries—for himself, Cakebread, and Fisher—and would go on to build two stables and a guest house on the ranch. He and his partner, Eric Haesloop, responded enthusiastically to the challenge, drawing on the expertise of their Bay Area firm. Inspired by the hilly landscape and the local vernacular, they proposed a 10,000-square-foot V-plan structure of two gabled wings, one for wine and the other for oil, which would share an expansive porch. Straw-bale and stone construction were considered before the architects settled on *pise* (an acronym for pneumatically impacted stabilized earth, which is mixed with one percent of Portland cement and sprayed onto a steel frame).

Client and contractor took a chance on *pise*, for it was more costly as a building material than stucco or wood (though less than stone) and had previously been used only for houses, not for a structure of this scale. But Hall accepted the uncertainty and higher expense in order to achieve the long-term benefits of energy efficiency, low maintenance, and a pleasing sense of earthiness and mass. Haesloop explains that "although two-foot-thick *pise* walls have no greater thermal resistance than two-by-four-inch studs, they transfer heat very slowly. As a result, the interior stays cool during hot summer days, and warms up during the cool nights." The mix preserves the natural color of the earth and, while still damp, it was scraped with a taut wire to create crisp edges and an interesting texture. This can be hosed down in the wine production areas; however, in the oil-pressing room, where the walls become coated with a fine oily mist, marmorino (plaster mixed with marble dust) was rubbed into the *pise* to provide a smoother, more easily cleaned surface.

Wine and oil were produced in earliest antiquity, and this building has an appropriately timeless quality. Outside and in, it is all of a piece; it serves as a portal to the wine caves hollowed from the hillside behind and is constructed from the excavated soil. The porch defines a shady outdoor room for wine pressing and loading the olive press, doubling as a welcoming space for arriving guests and receptions. Unlike some of the showier Napa wineries, the power and beauty of Long Meadow Ranch are as organic as its products.

The architects designed the production areas for maximum efficiency. Concrete floors and galvanized steel corners withstand the impact of forklifts. Hoses can be run inside from the porch through low wall openings, and outlets for power, compressed air and water are grouped on easily cleaned aluminum wall plates. Racks and trays are positioned to reduce clutter. The structure is exposed throughout. Recycled timbers from a bridge were used for the beams and trusses, and plywood ceilings are stained the color of red wine. Stairs lead up from the entry hall to oak-floored offices with fir wainscots. The same armatures of recycled steel are employed throughout, supporting high-intensity holophane work lights in the warehouse, and a similar fixture with attached halogen pin spots in the offices. Another link between upstairs and downstairs is the perforated metal guard rail around the desk-top electronic equipment which was inspired by the protective screens on the olive presses.

Natural light is used as a precious resource, for skylights have to be rationed in a building with no air conditioning. The largest of three is placed so that it provides the staircase, clerical and executive office with light that Haesloop describes as "magical and mysterious, changing in color and intensity through the day, with the earth walls as an absorbent canvas." The comfortable ambiance of the offices is enhanced by a fireplace with a massive surround of rammed earth—which has a more varied texture than *pise*— and by the way the trusses fan out like the spokes of a fan where the gables converge.

"The building is a statement of what we are about, and impresses people who are important to us," says Hall. "The mass of material shuts out sound and generates an extraordinary sense of tranquillity."

Not open to the public. Tel. +1 707 963 4555. 1775 Whitehall Lane, St. Helena, California. www.longmeadowranch.com

STORAGE

PRESS

FORKLIFT

2500 GAL

2500 GAL

1000 GAL

2500 GAL

4500 GAL

1500 GAL

1500 GAL

2500 GAL

3000 GAL

FERMENTATION

LAB

ENTRY
HALL

CRUSH PORCH

CRUSHER

PRESS

OLIVE OIL
PROCESSING

STORAGE

CRUSHER

HOPPER

BOTTLING

BOTTLING

SCALE

0   20m

STRYKER SONOMA WINERY

ALEXANDER VALLEY, CALIFORNIA

Nielsen: Schuh Architects, 2000–2002

The entrepreneurial spirit that has propelled California into the major league of winemaking is exemplified by this modest new venture and the dedication of the couple who run it. Karen Maley worked for Gallo's international marketing division; her husband, Craig MacDonald, in sales; they left to purchase a 31-acre estate on the road leading north to Geyserville. There they replanted the vines, and opened their own boutique winery, which is named for investor Patricia Stryker. Together, they researched fifty wineries, making notes on what they liked and didn't like, down to the smallest details.

"A lot of wineries are intimidating, making visitors feel like teenagers at their father's country club," says Maley. "Our goal was to be sophisticated and approachable, creating the winery we always wanted to go to, with production at the heart of the operation. It would be designed to handle small-lot production, and the building would be contemporary, to reflect the character of the operation, but with links to the traditional feelings people have about wine."

Alexander Valley is a small-scale farming community, with none of the wealth and glitter of Napa Valley, though its grapes are highly esteemed. In this setting, a pretentious building would be as jarring as gold lamé at a hoe-down. Maley wanted a modern take on a barn—something that would fit in and please the neighbors—but sensitively designed, so that visitors

would pick up on the quality and think, "anyone who builds like this must make great wine." She knew she had to find the right architects, trusting them to realize her vision, and she picked the local husband-and-wife partnership of Richard Schuh and Amy Nielsen—in part for an imaginative proposal they had made to Gallo, but chiefly because their home office embodied everything she wanted in the winery.

From the road, the low structure hugs the ground and merges into the hills behind, revealing little more than two gables, connected by a roof, and a curved stone retaining wall. Close-up, the familiar barn imagery begins to unravel. What appeared as slatted wood is seen to be concrete louvers set into slender steel columns, which provide shade but reveal glimpses of the winemaking process. Rubble stone walls tie the building to the land, poured concrete walls express the core, and the roofs are covered in standing-seam copper. The rhyolite stone from Napa is overall a warm neutral gray, but contains many different tones—including the putty brown that's used for stucco on the wood-framed section.

Visitors walk beneath a pergola, past the production area, to the glass-walled tasting room with its tall, airy canopy and wrap-around deck. The broad gable covers the tank room at the south end, and grapes are gravity-fed into the tanks from a loading dock to the rear. Production is currently 5000 cases a year, with a capacity of 20,000. The tasting room is a light-filled space that offers panoramic views over the estate and through an inner window into

the barrel room, which is embedded in the hillside. A delicate steel frame supports the Douglas fir vault. The open hearth and curved bar appear to float on the polished expanse of the concrete floor, which is stained to resemble vintage leather. An artisanal steel gate encloses the VIP tasting room within the sales area.

The building itself was handcrafted, for the architects drew it the old-fashioned way, without recourse to CAD. They persuaded their clients to accept raw concrete and exposed steel as a foil to wood and warm tones. The whole design was a balancing act, which combines form and function, production and hospitality, protection and openness. "As you experience the building you understand the functional relationships," says Schuh. "We avoided the temptation to use towers and other romantic but irrelevant forms. We composed the essential elements of the building without adding anything extraneous. They didn't want to overwhelm the site with buildings—they could always add storage elsewhere. Energy conservation was a priority. By lowering the barrel room into the earth we reduced the profile of the building, permitted gravity flow from tanks, and added thermal mass. The roof is heavily insulated, the building is naturally cooled at night, and natural lighting reduces power consumption and heat build-up."

Open daily. Tours by appointment. Tel: +1 707 433 1944. 5110 Highway 128, Geyserville, California. www.strykersonoma.com

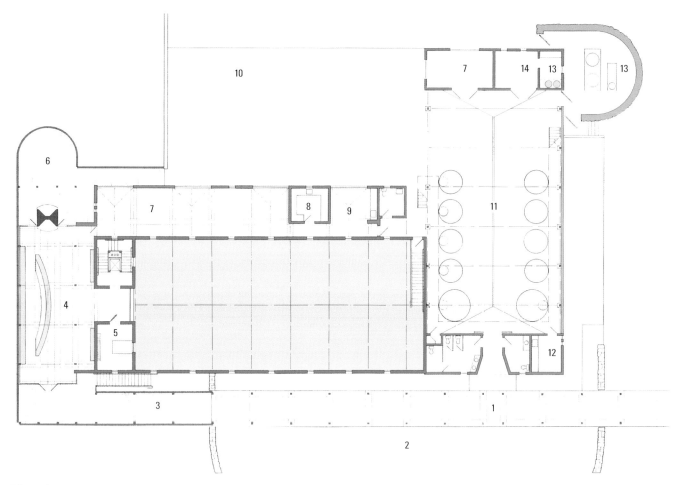

Main level floor plan

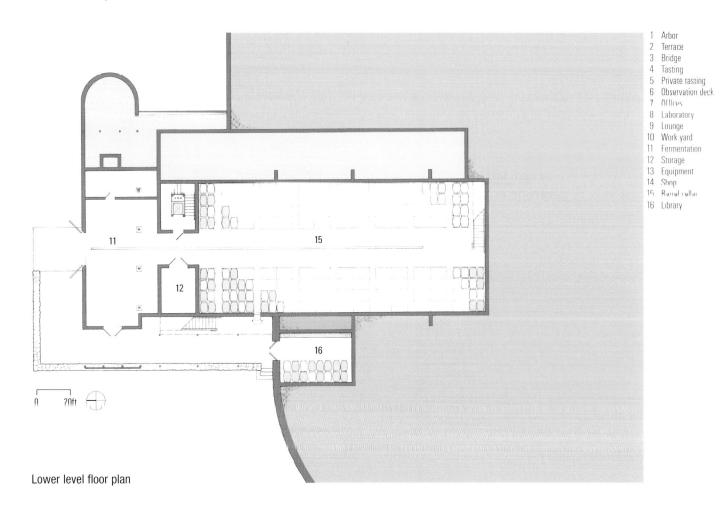

1   Arbor
2   Terrace
3   Bridge
4   Tasting
5   Private tasting
6   Observation deck
7   Offices
8   Laboratory
9   Lounge
10 Work yard
11 Fermentation
12 Storage
13 Equipment
14 Shop
15 Barrel cellar
16 Library

0   20ft

Lower level floor plan

SHAW & SMITH

**JBG Architects with Chris Connell
1999–2000**

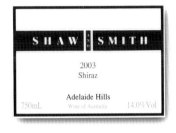

Natural beauty and a temperate climate make the Adelaide Hills an ideal place for winemaking (especially for Sauvignon Blanc, Chardonnay, and Pinot Noir); grapes were planted here as early as 1839. In the early 1980s, the industry took off, and the authorities set a limit on the number and size of new wineries to preserve the quality of the environment. Martin Shaw, a winemaker who had previously worked at Petaluma and in Europe, established a winery with his cousin, Michael Hill Smith, in 1989 and they relocated to this former stud farm ten years later.

"We didn't want to build a whacking great tin shed out here because what happens if you grow out of it?' says Shaw. "You have to build another big shed or extend it, which doesn't look good." The practical, low-cost solution was a row of interconnecting modular units, each 33 feet wide, with an insulated double skin of colorbond on the outside and easy-to-clean zinc on the inner face. There's a fluid flow of space within the production areas, which occupy all the bays to the rear of the office and hospitality areas.

From afar, the seven slate-gray gables resemble a minimalist artwork or a row of Monopoly houses. The lawn and vineyards slope gently down to a lake,

a clump of gum trees and a distant prospect of Mount Lofty. The original five-bay façade is faced with glass and shaded by a steel pergola that serves as an outdoor room for entertaining. Two blank-faced modules were seamlessly added to accommodate an increase in production, but the winery is only half-way toward its mandated ceiling of 150,000 cases, so there may be more bays to come.

Shaw and Smith collaborated with Jamie Gladigau on the architecture, and with interior designer Chris Connell on the understated banqueting/meeting room and tasting area. Splashes of orange and ochre animate the entry area, where a tall window frames the barrel store beyond, and a clear slot in a translucent glass partition provides a peep hole from the offices, eliminating the need for a reception desk. "We believe a winery visit is about winning hearts and minds, and we've gotten a lot of press coverage," says Smith. "We don't receive a lot of visitors—70 on a weekend is typical—but it's nice to hold a party for 30. Though the building is inexpensive, it expresses the character of the lighter, more sophisticated premium wines we produce."

Weekend tastings by appointment. Tel: +61 8 8398 0500. Lot 4, Jones Road, Balhannah, South Australia. www.shawandsmith.com

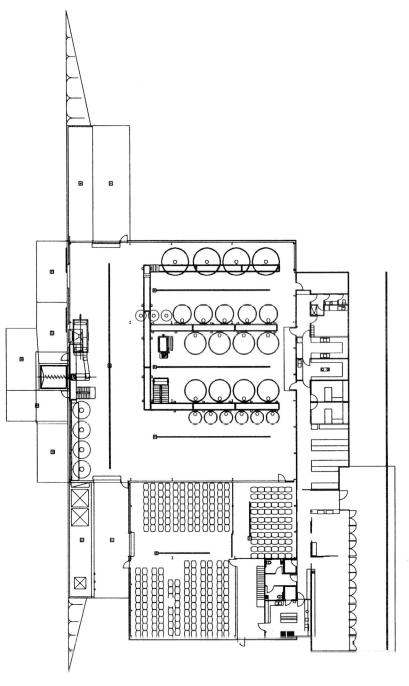

BLACK BARN VINEYARDS

HAWKES BAY, NEW ZEALAND

Andy Coltart with Peter Tatham
2002–2003

In 1994, entrepreneur Andy Coltart joined Saatchi NZ chairman Kim Thorp to establish this small premium winery, which harvests 20 acres of grapes and makes 6000 cases of wine at Lombardi, the adjoining property. The complex was meticulously planned, step-by-step, as a destination, with four luxurious guest cottages, an outdoor amphitheater for summer concerts, a farmers market within a circle of shade trees, and finally a cellar-door restaurant, designed by Coltart with help from Peter Tatham, an interior designer.

At Black Barn, the emphasis is on hospitality. A tasting room and restaurant are set on a knoll, flanked by wings containing the kitchen, offices and a lab, with a small art gallery enclosing the fourth side of a narrow courtyard. Crisp forms and white trim on black provide a sophisticated abstraction of the rural vernacular. Behind the bar is an expansive dining area with pale gray walls and a lantern. Windows wrap around on three sides, framing the vineyards and folding back to give the rear section the character of an open porch. Beyond, steps lead down to an enclosed space within the vineyard, shaded by straw mats and a vine-clad pergola. There's a lovely play of shadows over the teak chairs and bare earth, and long vistas down rows of grapes to distant buildings.

The stylish simplicity of Black Barn epitomizes the quality of wine and cuisine, furnishes a strong identity, and positions the company in the market. "It's all about lifestyle—wine, food, and song," says Coltart. "The cellar door is our public face. The amphitheatre provides the music. We wanted the buildings to be timeless and classical."

Open daily. Tel: +64 6 877 7985. Black Barn Road, RD 12, Havelock North, Hawkes Bay.
www.blackbarn.com

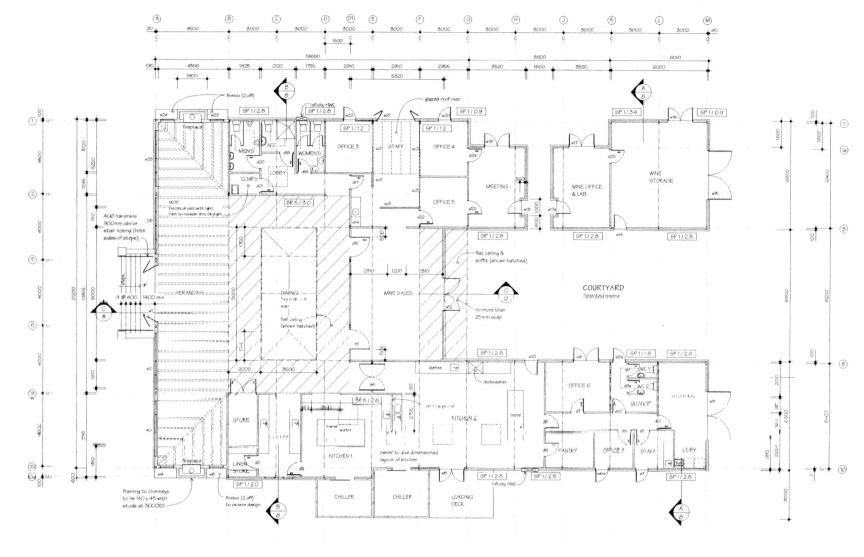

NEW AND EARLIER VINTAGES

ARGENTINA

AUSTRALIA

AUSTRIA

USA

CANADA

CHILE

ITALY

NEW ZEALAND

SPAIN

BODEGA O. FOURNIER

VALLE DE UCO, ARGENTINA
Bormida & Yanzón, 2003–2006

In this ambitious new venture by a winemaking family from Burgos, Spain, a double ramp carries trucks onto the roof of a massive tank room for gravity loading, with a barrel cellar below. Four concrete columns support a projecting steel canopy, which is clad like an airplane wing, and shades a central office and lab. A plaza and visitors' center are to be built to the rear.

Visits by appointment. Tel: +54 2622 451 579. Calle Los Indios s/n, 5567 La Consulta, Mendoza. www.bodegasofournier.com

DOMAINE CHANDON

YARRA VALLEY, VICTORIA, AUSTRALIA
Allen Jack & Cottier, 1987–1990

The design of this winery enhances both linear production sequences and a sense of theatrics. Visitors descend through the production areas that are embedded in a hillside to view the press and fermenting tanks (which extend outdoors to the rear), the bottling line, and the riddling hall (riddle means to turn the bottles of sparking wine), progressing to a stair landing and look-out across the Yarra Valley beneath a great arched vault. From outside, the arch of the tasting room dissolves into a lightweight, vine-covered pergola, with a restaurant to one side.

Open daily. Tel: +61 3 9739 1110. Maroondah Highway, Coldstream, Victoria. www.domainechandon.com.au

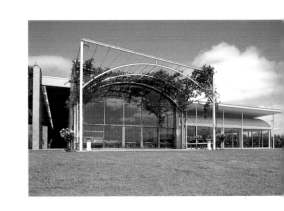

NATIONAL WINE CENTRE OF AUSTRALIA

ADELAIDE, SOUTH AUSTRALIA, AUSTRALIA
Grieve & Gillett and Cox Richardson, 1997–2001

A showcase for the Australian wine industry that includes a wine bar, meeting areas and informative exhibits on the history and techniques of winemaking. A ramp leads up the side of the building, which is clad with staves to evoke a wine barrel, and the three levels are linked by an elliptical skylit atrium.

Open daily. Tel: +61 8 8222 9222. Botanic Road, Adelaide. www.wineaustralia.com.au

PENFOLDS MAGILL ESTATE WINERY

ADELAIDE, SOUTH AUSTRALIA, AUSTRALIA
Allen Jack & Cottier, 1992–1995

A heritage site with 25 acres of vines dating back to the original settlement of 1844, which produces a single-estate Shiraz. Keith Cottier upgraded the old winery buildings, housing the premium brands tasting room in the former spirits distillery, which retains two dramatic pot stills. His minimalist new restaurant of steel, glass, and concrete forms a transparent bridge between winery, vineyards, and the spectacular view, making Penfolds a destination.

Open daily. Tel: +61 8 8301 5569. 78 Penfolds Road, Magill. www.penfolds.com

WEINGUT FRED LOIMER

LANGENLOIS, AUSTRIA
Andreas Burghardt, 2000–2001

A near neighbor of Loisium, set on a hillside off a rustic lane. An L-plan tasting room/art gallery and office of concrete with black render bracket a grassy courtyard, complementing the existing production facilities (for twelve quality wines) and ancient cellars.

Visits by appointment. Tel: +43 2734 2239 3. Haindorfer Vogelweg 23. www.loimer.at

WEINGUT POLZ

STYRIA, AUSTRIA
g2plus Grabensteiner Architects, 2001–2002

Martina Grabensteiner added a tasting room to the venerable Polz winery, whose steeply terraced vineyards command sweeping views over the pastoral Styrian countryside. Empty bottles stacked in a vitrine filter the light in a stone-framed space that's set into the vine-clad hillside.

Open daily. Tel: +43 3453 2301. Grassnitzberg 54A, Spielfeld. www.polz.co.at

WEINGUT SCHILHAN

STYRIA, AUSTRIA
g2plus Grabensteiner Architects, 2005

A ground-up winery, located a few kilometers from Polz and a world away in its radical expression. It's nicknamed "Crocodile Rock" for its profile and for its owner, Willy Schilhan, who is known as "The Elvis from Jägerberg." The architect has integrated the building in the landscape by burying the production areas and putting the offices and hospitality areas with their sweeping roofs on top.

Open daily. Tel: +43 3 453 6094. Kranach 8, Gamlitz. www.weingut-schilhan.at

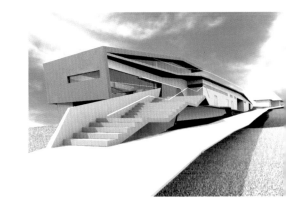

ARTESA

NAPA VALLEY, CALIFORNIA
Domingo Triay and Earl R. Bouligny, 1999–2001

This 127,000-square-foot facility is built into a quarry and is almost entirely concealed by a grass berm. Stairs and fountains lead up to the entrance at the top of the pyramid, where tasting and display areas are ranged around a pergola-shaded courtyard similar to that at Legaris. The production areas below are naturally insulated and are designed for the production of small lots of premium wine.

Open daily. Tel: +1 707 224 1668. 1345 Henry Road, Napa, California.
www.artesawinery.com

CHAPPELLET

NAPA VALLEY, CALIFORNIA
Collaborative venture, 1968–1969

A family winery that introduced modern architecture to the area, and remains as striking and functional as when it was new. Donn and Molly Chappellet collaborated with engineer Dick Keith and two artist friends, Ed Moses and Ed Ruscha, to create a pyramid from three triangles of CorTen steel, lit from glass slots between them. It encloses 17,000 square feet and was built, 35 years ago, for $16 a square foot! Within, it's like a great barn, with a wooden staircase ascending to an office and three terraces at the apex. The plan is incorporated into the wine label.

Visits by appointment. Tel: +1 800 494 6379. 1581 Sage Canyon Road, St Helena, California. www.chappellet.com

HESS COLLECTION

NAPA VALLEY, CALIFORNIA
Beat A.H. Jordi, 1989

"Two passions under one roof," is how Donald Hess describes the remodeling of a century-old winery to house state-of-art production facilities and his exemplary collection of modern and contemporary art works. Jordi, a fellow Swiss, created a dramatic, light-filled stair hall to link two buildings, and you glimpse the barrels and tanks as you ascend and walk into the galleries.

Open daily. Tel: +1 707 255 1144. 4411 Redwood Road, Napa, California. www.hesscollection.com

ROSHAMBO

Jacques Ullman, 2002

Naomi Johnson Brilliant realized her grandfather's dream of creating a winery, after studying art, and she commissioned this boldly contemporary trio of buildings from a seasoned professional. "His initial drawings resembled Quonset huts—I came up with the idea of a wave vault for the tasting room office, putting a little cap over Mt Helena, which dominates the view". Its stucco and glass contrasts with the stainless and stucco tank room, and the steel-clad barrel room. The buildings cleverly exploit the drop from entry to crush pad, and Brilliant has created a welcoming atmosphere and display area for her artist chums.

Open daily. Tel: +1 707 431 2051. 3000 Westside Road, Healdsburg, California.
www.roshambowinery.com

LE CLOS JORDAN

NIAGARA PENINSULA, CANADA

Gehry Partners, 2000–

When it is finally realized, this could be the world's most spectacular winery: a silvery cloud hovering over gently sloping vineyards in a forest clearing. A glade of curved wood beams rise from the cellar to support the roof of a great hall, from which you can glimpse every stage of production, from loading to bottling, and tour each area along skylit canyons that lead to the tasting room. Gehry and Edwin Chan, the project designer, planned a small working winery of softly curving white plaster walls and an undulating metal roof that will emerge from the landscape and reflect the sky. It will operate on multiple levels, above and below grade, to take advantage of the natural gravity flow within the winemaking process.

VIÑA ODFJELL

SANTIAGO, CHILE
Laurence Odfjell, 2001

In building his own winery, Odfjell explored ideas of concealment and interlocking spaces that he would amplify at Matetic. Here, the production areas are mostly buried in hillside; offices and a tasting room are set forward to provide a belvedere looking over the vineyards below and out to the cordillera. A grassy courtyard with a massive concrete pergola is set in the angle between.

Visits by appointment. Tel: +56 02 811 1538. Camino Viejo a Valparaiso, Padre Hurtado, Santiago. www.odfjellvineyards.cl

BODEGA LOS MAQUIS

COLCHAGUA VALLEY, CHILE
Saez Joannon Arquitectos and Juan Ignacio Lopez, 2002–2003

A rigorous, steel-framed concrete and glass box, handsomely detailed and flooded with natural light. A family conglomerate wanted quality construction for large scale production (up to 1.5 million liters) of premium red wine in seven varietals. The original intention was to leave the tank room and mezzanine loading gallery open at the sides, though shaded by elegant metal brise soleils. But cold wind and rain off the Andes made it uncomfortable for the workers so glass was added.

FEUDI DI SAN GREGORIO

CAMPANIA, ITALY
Hikaru Mori, 2003–2004

A splashy standout among modest wineries that are beginning to regain the reputation this region enjoyed in ancient times. The sleek metal-clad buildings showcase ambitious wines and include Marenna, an acclaimed restaurant.

Open daily. Tel: +39 0823 986 611. Sorbo Serpico. www.feudi.it

LA ROCCA DI FRASSINELLO

TUSCANY, ITALY
Renzo Piano Building Workshop, 2004–2005

A prestigious collaboration between DBR Lafite and Castellare di Castellina. Project architect Massimo Alvisi worked with Piano's office to create a cathedral-like space on a hilltop site. Tanks are ranged around a square stepped barrel room: a square within a square of raw concrete. Despite the grandeur of the structure, which has a rooftop plaza and glass pavilion for events, production will be limited to 1500 cases a year.

Visits by appointment. Tel: +39 0577 742 903. Podere Frassinello, Gavorrano. www.castellare.it isodi@tin.it

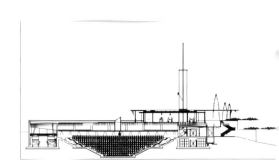

SPY VALLEY WINES

BLENHEIM, NEW ZEALAND
Bevin & Slessor and Cedric Edwards of CEDCO, 2002–2003

Steel-framed, insulated panel construction, faced with cedar boards and a flat roof with angled skylights. Walls are cut away in places to reveal panels and narrow windows; dot-dash openings spell out the name, which was inspired by the proximity of a satellite communications monitoring base. To break up the mass, the open fermenting tanks for Pinot Noir are located in one two-bay building, and the tanks for Sauvignon Blanc in a taller, three-bay structure. A partially-covered "street" runs between them, providing protected space for loading and pressing. The tasting and reception rooms with offices above are contained within a wing faced with slats over glass, which draws the eye through to a terrace on the far side and the vineyard beyond. The landscaping weaves the winery together with the vineyards, which extend away to misty hills.

Visits by appointment. Tel: +64 3 572 9840. 37 Lake Timara Road, RD 6.
www.spyvalleywine.co.nz

PEREGRINE WINERY

CENTRAL OTAGO, NEW ZEALAND
Architecture Workshop, 2003–2004

Everything under one roof—a torqued, translucent canopy that extends 460 feet to protect the buildings from sun and snow in this, the world's most southerly wine-growing region. The gentle curve plays off the rugged landscape and a historic woolshed, providing an unforgettable image of this linear winery. Tastings are held in the extended barrel room, which is embedded in the ground, and visitors can then stroll the terrace above.

Open daily. Tel: +64 3 442 4000. Kawarau Gorge Road, RD1, Queenstown.
www.peregrinewines.co.nz

VILLA MARIA ESTATE

AUCKLAND, NEW ZEALAND
Hamish Cameroun, 2002–2005

Located in a volcanic crater just minutes from the international airport, this sprawling complex is designed as a state-of-art production facility and a destination, with an ambitious tour program, conference center, hotel and restaurant. Villa Maria draws grapes from the major regions to make a wide variety of award-winning wines. Award-winning architecture, and a great introduction to New Zealand winemaking.

Open daily. Tel: +64 9 255 0000. 118 Montgomerie Road, Mangere. www.villamaria.co.nz

CVNE VIÑA RÉAL

RIOJA ALAVESA, SPAIN
Philippe Mazières, 2002–2004

The bottling plant is faced in cedar boards and adjoins a hilltop rotunda 200 feet in diameter, faced in stained pine to resemble a giant barrel. Trucks arrive at the upper level, grapes are loaded into small steel tanks which are then transferred to large steel tanks by a crane arm that rotates from a central pyramid of beams supporting the skylight. From here, the wine is gravity-fed into concrete tanks on the floor below and then into barrels that are arranged at the center beneath a glass disc. The glass and sycamore tasting room opens off the upper level; tunnels lead off from the lower level.

Visits by appointment. Tel: +34 945 625 255. Ctra Logrono–Laguardia. www.cvne.com

BODEGAS FAUSTINO

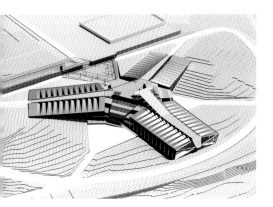

RIBERA DEL DUERO, SPAIN
Foster & Partners, 2003–2007

A major new winery for Grupo Faustino, one of the leading winemakers of La Rioja, with storage capacity for 5000 barrels and a million bottles of high-quality wine. Three "petals" radiate from a core of shared service and social areas, and the reinforced concrete frame structure will be partly buried in the ground. A first-class restaurant and banqueting facilities are planned, and a 45-room hotel will be added at a later date.

Visits by appointment after summer 2007. Gumiel de Hizan. info@bodegasfaustino.es

LOPEZ DE HEREDIA

LA RIOJA, SPAIN
Zaha Hadid, 2003–2004

Hadid won the Pritzker Prize for her mastery of unique geometries and dynamic volumes, and this modest addition gives an old winery a new signature and adds to the region's concentration of audacious architecture. Planes of gold-toned metal embrace a century-old timber pavilion in a form that suggests the cone-shaped flask from which Spaniards sometimes drink their wine.

Visits by appointment. Tel: +34 941 31 02 44. Avda. De Vizcaya 3, Haro. www.lopezdeheredia.com

BODEGAS PROTOS

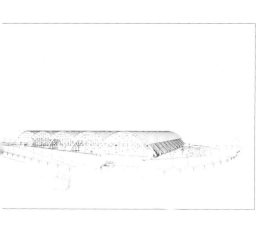

RIBERA DEL DUERO, SPAIN
Richard Rogers Partnership, 2004–2006

Rogers has designed a one-million-liter winery for a long-established firm on a triangular plinth at the base of the Peñafiel castle hill. Five interlinked parabolic vaults clad in terracotta tiles are supported on timber arches, to shade the production facilities; a subterranean barrel cellar is linked by a tunnel to the old winery. A sunken garden brings natural light to the lower-level offices. The ground-hugging forms are a reinterpretation of the rural vernacular.

Visits by appointment after February 2006. Tel: +34 983 878011. Peñafiel (Valladolid). bodega@bodegasprotos.com

ACKNOWLEDGMENTS

Wine is synonymous with pleasure and hospitality, and this book is a tribute to the dedicated winemakers who welcomed me and explained their craft. It is also a celebration of the diverse ways in which architects accommodate and express that craft. Peggy Loar, the director of Copia, inspired the idea for the book, and Scott Johnson gave me the insights that got it started, and offered helpful comments on the draft. Janice Robinson and Frank Prial offered encouragement and opened doors. Paul Latham and Alessina Brooks gave the project their unstinted support, Darren Heberle and Jason Phillips did an exemplary job of design, and Robyn Beaver steered the book to completion with unfailing patience and skill.

My greatest debt is to Erhard Pfeiffer, a photographer with the eye of an artist, who signed up early for the quest and secured memorable images around the world.

—MW

This book is dedicated to my wine-loving father who introduced me to photography and who would have loved to see this book. It is also dedicated to my dear mother who enjoys the travel more than the wine. Last not least I want to thank Cecy for her love and patience and my children for who they are.

—EP

© Aiken Weiss

Michael Webb grew up in London, and now lives in Los Angeles, in the Richard Neutra apartment that Charles and Ray Eames once called home. His 20 books on architecture and design include *Art/Invention/House*, *Brave New Houses: Adventures in Southern California Living*, and *Modernism Reborn: Mid Century Modern American Houses*. Earlier titles include brief monographs on Ingo Maurer, George Nelson, and Richard Sapper; an anthology of photographs, *It's a Great Wall!* (The Images Publishing Group); as well as architectural monographs and a guide to the architecture of L.A. As a contributing writer to *Architectural Digest*, *Frame*, and *Travel + Life*, and a regular contributor to *The Architectural Review*, he travels the world in search of new material.

Erhard training for the next adventure
© Marc Pfeiffer 2005

Erhard Pfeiffer is one of the foremost photographers of architecture, interiors and hospitality. His images have graced the covers of numerous leading publications and books. To see more of his photographs and a list of published work visit www.erhardpfeiffer.com.

When he is not busy travelling the world he enjoys the beach near his Dean Nota designed home in Venice, California. There he can be seen rollerblading with his dogs, trying to keep up with his children Marc and Kira.

All photography is © Erhard Pfeiffer, except pages 51–53 courtesy Gruppo Mezzacorona; pages 55–57 © Robert Herbst; pages 59–61 courtesy Gehry Partners; pages 71–75 courtesy Ca'Marcanda; pages 99–101 © Lorenzo Mussi, courtesy Cantina Ghidossi; pages 135–141 © Paul Warchol, courtesy Mission Hill Family Estate; pages 171–175 © Cesar Rubio, courtesy Long Meadow Ranch; pages 183–185 © Michael Webb [exterior], courtesy Shaw & Smith [interior].

Page 194 (bottom); page 195 (top, middle and bottom); page 196 (top), page 198 (top), page 199 (bottom), and page 201 (top) all © Michael Webb.

Page 194 (top) courtesy Bormida & Yanzón, page 194 (middle) courtesy g3plus Grabnowzelmer Architects, page 196 (bottom) courtesy Codorniu; page 197 (top) courtesy Chappellet; page 197 (bottom) courtesy Hess Collection; page 198 (bottom) courtesy Gehry Partners; page 199 (top) courtesy Laurence Odfjell; page 200 (top) courtesy Feudi di San Gregorio; page 200 (bottom) courtesy Renzo Piano Building Workshop; page 201 (bottom) © Patrick Reynolds, courtesy Architecture Workshop; page 202 (top) courtesy Villa Maria Estate; page 203 (top) courtesy Foster & Partners; page 203 (middle) courtesy Zaha Hadid Architects; page 203 (bottom) courtesy Richard Rogers Partnership.